Sustainable Jewellery

Julia Manheim

A & C Black • London

To my mother, who kept everything,
and my father, who gave everything away.

First published in Great Britain in 2009
A & C Black Publishers Limited
36 Soho Square
London W1D 3QY
www.acblack.com

ISBN: 978-0-7136-8344-8
Copyright © 2009 text Julia Manheim

Julia Manheim has asserted her right under the Copyright,
Design and Patents Act, 1988, to be identified as the author
of this work.

CIP Catalogue records for this book are available from the
British Library and the U.S. Library of Congress.

Book design: Susan McIntyre
Cover design: James Watson
Commissioning Editor: Susan James
Managing Editor: Sophie Page
Copy Editor: Julian Beecroft

Typeset in 10.5 on 14pt Myriad Light

Printed and bound in China

This book is produced using paper that is made from wood
grown in managed, sustainable forests. It is natural,
renewable and recyclable. The logging and manufacturing
processes conform to the environmental regulations of the
country of origin.

FRONTISPIECE *Line of Light*, Georgina Edwards, 2002. Striplight.
Photo: Trefor Ball.

Sustainable
Jewellery

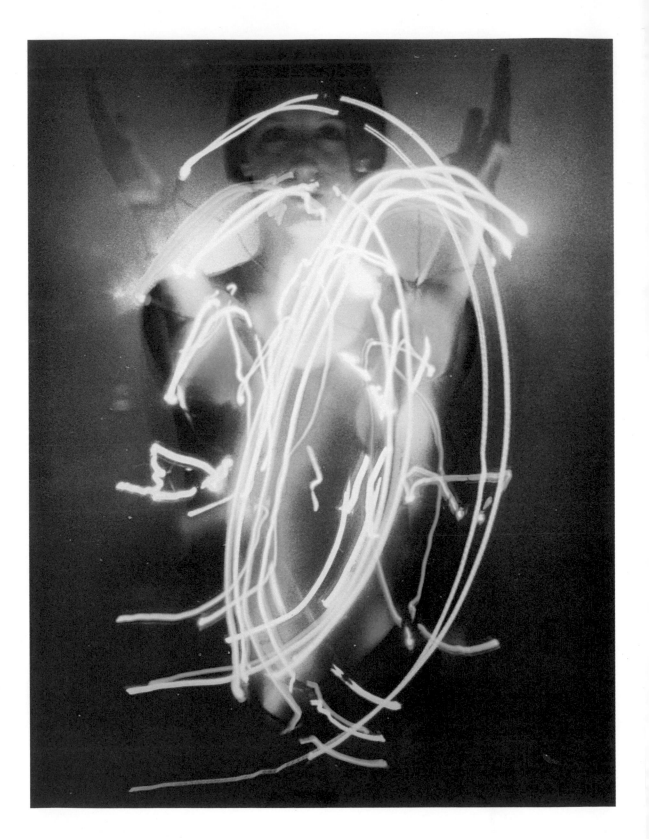

Contents

Acknowledgements

I would like to thank everyone who has helped and encouraged me in the writing of this book, in particular: Caroline Broadhead, Elisabeth Holder, Ros Conway, Paul Derrez, Mathieu Obers, Ken Taylor, Vanessa Hill, Julie Westbury, Johanna Dahm, Craig Isaac and Anthony Coleman.

I also want to say a big thank you to all the jewellers, artists and designers who have been so generous in giving me information and allowing me to publish images of their work, including; graduates, undergraduates and staff of BA Honours Jewellery at Middlesex University and MA Goldsmithing, Silversmithing, Metalwork and Jewellery at the Royal College of Art,

I am grateful to the School of Arts & Education at Middlesex University for a grant to help with the research needed to write this book.

Foreword

As you enter the side gate of Julia Manheim's studio in South London, you encounter a wall of wire containers filled with hundreds of translucent plastic, 'disposable' milk containers. The mass of redundant bottles has a startling impact. Practically, they act as a wind break and privacy screen; they are also indicative of the change, over the last few decades, in the way milk is packaged; and in addition, they refer back to the building's former use as a milk depot, which Julia and her partner, architect Ken Taylor, converted to its present use as apartments and studios. This economic and pertinent use of materials is characteristic of Julia's approach.

Although trained as a jeweller, and having gained an international reputation for this work, Julia has resolutely and continuously set wider and wider frameworks to work within. Her work includes jewellery pieces, as well as objects for dance, performance and sculpture and more recently, work within architecture. Frequently, the work is made in collaboration with architects, choreographers and other artists. Over more than 30 years, her remarkable journey has given rise to an impressive body of work, which steers a clear, unique path through different disciplines, materials and contexts, from which this

Milk Container Wall, Julia Manheim/Ken Taylor, 2006. Plastic milk containers, steel gabions. Photo: Anthony Coleman

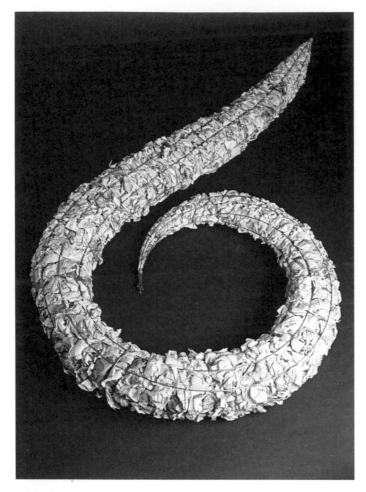

Rough Stuff, Julia Manheim, 1990. *Guardian* newspaper, wire, (l) 238 cm (8 ft).
Photo: Ed Barber

book has emerged. The constants throughout are a quality of wit, an appropriateness of materials and how they are found and used, and an outstanding sense of colour, light and space.

Her concern for the thoughtless disposal of materials emerged in the early 1970s, finding herself amid an accumulation of piles of *Guardian* newspapers, a lack of recycling facilities and an instinctive dislike of anything going to waste. Her ability to see this as a positive opportunity meant that the newspapers became both material and subject matter for a range of work that was to continue over the following twenty years. The works in paper developed alongside other projects, but they illustrate the expansion of scale and intention behind Julia's work during that period.

She has been lead artist on several architectural projects, producing work for a particular building or site herself, as well as acting in the role of advisor to commission other artists. Julia's considerable contribution to art integrated with architecture has been recognised in an RIBA Art for Architecture Award for the Norden Farm Centre for the Arts project in 1998. It is in this context that sustainability has become a key motivation.

In 2002, Julia marked a walk around the town of Wolverton, Milton Keynes, with a series of tiles set into the pavement at strategic points. These were made up of discarded objects, collected by Julia and local residents, which were then embedded into terrazzo tiles. When sanded down, the new surface revealed a slice through the buried objects. The collection of combs, toys, toothbrushes, Lego bricks, etc. were chosen for their form and colour, so that some were easy to recognise, but others needed further thought to identify. By making permanent what is seen to be transient or throwaway, and by making visible what society wants to put out of sight, the value of these 'out of date' objects could be reassessed. Julia created premature archaeology, a 21st-century museum underfoot.

2-Peaks Bracelet, Julia Manheim, 1985. Painted newspaper.
Photo: John McCarthy

BELOW *Objects and Illusions*, Julia Manheim, 2007. Recycling bin with locating panel; featuring 'smile' recycled plastic samples.
Still-life photography: Anthony Coleman;
print & wrap: Artmongers.
Photo: Anthony Coleman

As lead artist on a schools project for Crawley Art and Architecture Programme, completed in 2007, Julia directly promoted the ethos of recycling at Thomas Bennett Community College, resurfacing the large plastic bins with images of ubiquitous found 'rubbish' such as telephone press pads, the undersides of plastic water bottles, postmen's red rubber bands and shredded paper. At each location point, there was a wall panel made up of the actual elements. This project was considered such a success that plans are afoot to extend this provision to other schools in West Sussex.

It is not unusual for an artist's concerns and ideas to be reworked and to surface in another piece of work, and this holds true in Julia's practice. Moreover, Julia's materials are more often than not scavenged or salvaged, and once work is returned from exhibitions it is then taken apart and reassessed as possible material for the next work. In this way, Julia's work and her materials have an embodied history; new pieces are born of old ones.

The BA Hons Jewellery programme at Middlesex University benefits from all of Julia's experience and knowledge. The programme is well-known for its imaginative and innovative use of materials and its broad interpretation of the subject. Julia has led projects on the subject of recycling, with titles such as *Junk2Jewellery* and *Old for New*, which have been highly influential in the way students look for potential in materials, their meanings and associations.

Jewellery can be made out of almost any material, and all materials reflect the passing of time in various ways. There is the time invested in the acquisition and production of materials themselves – some, such as metals, gemstones or plastics require enormous industrial activity, while others, such as daisies for a chain, require very little; there is the time taken in designing and fashioning the materials into objects; there is also the lifespan of these objects as either useful or desirable; and finally, after 'object-hood', there are the continuing lives of these materials, whether they are recycled, reused or buried as landfill.

At this point in our history, Western societies are producing such mountains of 'waste' – short-life, obsolete products, often made using sophisticated materials and processes – that artists and designers arguably have a greater choice of second-hand than virgin materials. Seeing potential in the overlooked is something artists and designers have long been accomplished in, and in *Sustainable Jewellery*, Julia has brought together examples of this sensibility in the work of contemporary jewellers as well as work with corresponding concerns by sculptors and furniture designers.

Julia Manheim is in a prime position to give this overview of sustainability in contemporary jewellery. *Sustainable Jewellery* is an informative guide to current thinking in this field, and the book, itself printed on recycled paper, is a modest step in the direction of promoting the minimal, moderate, responsible use of materials.

Caroline Broadhead

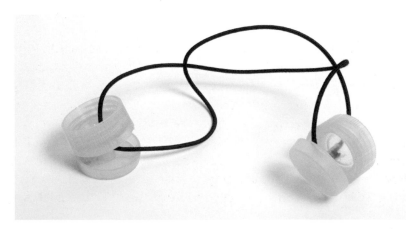

Eco Necklace, Julia Manheim, 2006. Ecover bottle tops, elastic cord.
Photo: Anthony Coleman

Introduction

'Sustainable' and 'sustainability' are relatively new terms which, being applicable to many complex subjects, including the environment, ecology and agriculture, have a tendency to lead to confusion. The Brundtland Commission, convened by the UN in 1983 to look into global environmental problems, later defined sustainable development as that which 'meets the needs of the present without compromising the ability of future generations to meet their own needs'. The emphasis is firmly on what can be done now to influence the legacy for the future, in terms of raw materials and ecosystems.

The word 'sustainability' sounds more familiar in the context of a vocabulary associated with architecture and building materials: timber from sustainable forests, thermal gain, green roofs and grey water. But that is on a grand scale; this book attempts to discover how it works on the much smaller scale of jewellery. My approach to the subject is as a teacher, maker and wearer of contemporary jewellery. I have adopted the method I would encourage in my students: to explore all avenues, to reference work from other areas of art and design and try to stretch your understanding of the theme by interpreting it with imagination, to look around for everyday examples, and to think laterally. Following this through, connections and parallels with the work of artists and designers outside the field of jewellery have been made throughout the book.

This is by no means an exhaustive survey of the idea of sustainability in jewellery, more of an enquiry into what it is and how it manifests itself. I have used examples which reinforce my own thoughts about sustainability and contemporary jewellery; therefore I have concentrated on interesting and innovative design, which may at times seem far-fetched, as it takes the notion of sustainability to the limit. Examples of jewellery from the 1970s onwards have been put forward as precedents for more recent sustainable jewellery. The work of students and emerging jewellers is shown alongside that of established designers, to encourage the reader to accept the

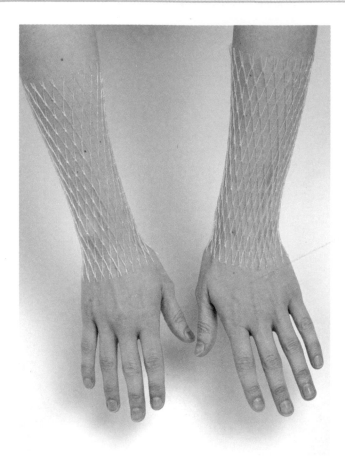

Bottle Protector Armpieces,
Julia Manheim, 2008. Nylon.
Photo: Anthony Coleman

notion that sustainability can be applied to everything, on all sorts of levels, and not just the obvious ones.

Jewellery has also been considered in the broadest sense of the word, embracing objects or images which relate to the body and are usually worn in some way, however fleetingly. It can refer to an object which is simply held in the hand, an image stamped or projected onto the body, or a photograph as the final piece. It could also be ready-made requiring little or no alteration in order to wear it.

In some cases, examples have been used of body-related work made by jewellers whose work has developed towards clothing, photography, or performance. Conversely, some examples are of jewellery made by people who have been trained in other disciplines such as engineering or painting. Other examples have been chosen for their jewel-like quality. By viewing both jewellery and sustainability in a broad way, it is hoped to inspire jewellery-making in the future that is both sustainable and imaginative.

The choice of materials used to make jewellery is important, allied with the way in which they are used. It is worth noting that all making uses energy and materials of some description, but it is the degree of damage caused which has to be weighed up. It is difficult to get accurate information on this and to judge the seriousness of the impact made. If jewellery has been made from discarded materials, but put together with non-ecological glue, can it still be called sustainable? Some jewellers and metalsmiths refuse to use so-called 'dirty' metals in their work, opting solely for second-hand metals or those which they have been given to believe come from reliable, environmentally sound sources. Others have found ways of replacing a forbidden material such as ivory with something which looks just like it. Vegetable ivory is the seed of a palm tree which can be harvested without cutting the tree down.

Ecological awareness may appear to be more advanced in some areas of art and design than others. Furniture designer Tejo Remy has revolutionised the way we think and feel about using furniture made from old clothing, just as the Campana brothers have also transformed industrial waste and cuddly toys into vibrant, desirable furniture.

Rag Chair, Tejo Remy (for droog), 1993. Fifteen bags of rags, steel strips, 60 x 60 x 110 cm.
Photo: Hans van der Mars

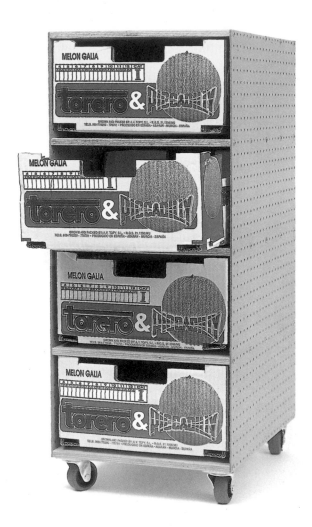

Torero, Michael Marriott,
1996. Birch ply, pegboard,
Spanish fruit crates.
Photo: David Cripps

British furniture designer Michael Marriott has been at the forefront of a collective sensibility which pokes fun at tradition, but also makes a virtue of creating something from nothing by incorporating found objects, materials or parts of other types of furniture into his work. The result is an appealing collage which has inspired others to think along similar lines.

Fashion designer, Martin Margiela, has based some of his past fashion collections on resizing old clothes to make them up to 200 per cent larger, and in the process has managed to make them 200 per cent more fashionable. In a different way, the Freitag brothers are making their mark on the collective design consciousness with practical, stylish bags sewn from used lorry tarpaulins, seatbelts and inner tubes. A high quality of design is evident throughout, from their entertaining website to the tower of ex-road-haulage containers which houses the Freitag shop in Zurich.

F14 Dexter bags, Freitag, 2008. Used lorry tarpaulins, rubber inner tubes, seatbelts. Photo: Isabel Truniger

There is also the question about making something worthless into a costly piece of jewellery through time and workmanship, and how that sits with the idea of sustainability. A current thread running through contemporary jewellery involves questioning the value of traditional jewellery forms and materials. This is often done by adding, taking away or superimposing traditional values onto materials which are not usually considered valuable in the context of jewellery. This is apparent in the way that jeweller Beppe Kessler mixes materials, often covering one with another, so that it is no longer possible to judge which is the more important or precious. For example, her *Rope of Pearls* necklace is a combination of pearls set into burnt balsa-wood beads which have been embroidered with black cotton, making the beads look as if they have been cross-hatched with a pen, or as though they have grown hair.

Rope of Pearls, Beppe Kessler,
2001. Burnt embroidered
balsa wood, pearls, cotton.
Photo: Taco Anema

This preoccupation could in itself be construed as a way of recycling, where old ideas are revisited and reinterpreted with the knowledge of hindsight. Currently, there is a thriving trade in the resale of 20th-century jewellery, not only in the big auction houses, antiques markets and fairs, but also online, via eBay and other websites. Buying second-hand, already-existing jewellery, whether it is antique or relatively contemporary, represents another form of recycling. It seems that an examination of jewellery, or indeed, any other subject from the point of view of sustainability immediately opens up a debate which raises more questions than it answers.

1 Old for New

THIS CHAPTER looks at different approaches to recycling existing jewellery to give it a second life and a new meaning. This might be achieved by altering it, wearing it differently from first time round, melting it down and reworking it, cutting it up, adding to it, covering it up, or casting it in another material. These are all methods of reinterpreting and valuing what is here already, rather than having to start from scratch. Developing a sensibility for looking at and seeing the potential in old things is a more holistic alternative to disposing of them, or creating something brand new.

Altering, changing or adding to jewellery is not a new or eco-friendly phenomenon. Until recently, it would probably not have been done in an attempt to save the environment, but it is an activity which has been around for centuries for other reasons. In her book *Jewels and Jewellery*, Clare Phillips devotes one section about antique jewellery to just this practice. From the 17th century onwards, it was not uncommon for the wealthy to change their jewellery by having stones reset and melting down the precious metal surrounds to fashion them differently. 'As a result of this practice it is only a very small proportion of jewellery from any period that has survived to the present day, although many pieces contain some elements, and certainly the raw materials, from a succession of earlier jewels'. During the early part of the 19th century, Prussians were encouraged to give up their gold for the war effort against Napoleon, in return for which they received the delicate, lacy, intricate pieces of black cast metal jewellery known as Berlin iron.

Today, even in our disposable culture, it is still commonplace for jewellers to be asked to convert clip-ons into pierced earrings, or to resize a wedding ring to fit another family member after the original wearer has died. These are alterations which give jewellery a second life, which is all to the good, but it is perhaps more interesting to consider ways in which jewellery can be reinvented by changing the sentiment or idea behind it. Having said that, it

Repaired sunglasses.
Photo: Anthony Coleman

is impossible to ignore the brilliant serendipity of a make-do-and-mend aesthetic. For instance, when a pair of spectacles has been mended with sticky tape, a safety pin or a piece of wire, the object is subtly changed both visually and in movement by these ad-hoc repairs, but is able to function again almost as good as new.

This brings to mind artist Richard Wentworth's take on his surroundings, his *Making Do and Getting By* photographs of makeshift notices or cobbled-together furniture found on the street, provide living proof that necessity is the mother of invention, often with hilarious results.

In 1996, Dutch jeweller Philip Sajet made a necklace out of a diverse selection of jewelled clasps, brooches and parts of other necklaces. Although each section comes from a different era they fit together very well in a surprisingly harmonious way.

Altering or reusing something which has sentimental value, when it may still be redolent of the wearer, could be emotionally painful and is not to be undertaken lightly. However, taking this step may provide the possibility of making the jewellery more wearable and giving it a new meaning – for example, *Siblings*, a chain necklace made by Lin Cheung out of broken jewellery that her brothers and sister had given her over the years to repair or remake. Cheung writes about the necklace in her book *Jewellery and Objects*. 'These chains that have ended up broken, knotted, tarnished and outdated seemed characteristic of each personality as we joined together to reminisce about childhood memories.'

Similarly, Otto Künzli's necklace made of 48 wedding rings sent to him by people each with their personal story to tell, makes a seemingly ordinary gold chain into an extraordinary piece of jewellery. The circle of a wedding ring is a symbol of eternal love, yet these rings had to be cut in order to make the chain. As Künzli was concerned to interfere with the rings as little as possible, he only cut every other one along the solder joint, which is always the weakest point, but every link bears witness as to why its owner was willing to give it away. Each ring came with a written explanation as to why it was no longer wanted. This makes a necklace of almost unbearable emotional weight, which in itself forms a continuous ring.

Sarah Baker's MA dissertation focused on donated jewellery, which was then sold in a variety of ways to raise funds for a hospice. During her research, she was given access to letters which had accompanied the donations, revealing the many different reasons why people had wanted to part with jewellery which was often of great sentimental value to them. In contrast to Otto Künzli's experience, none of the wedding rings sent in to

Siblings, necklace,
Lin Cheung, 2003. Silver, fine silver, gold.
Photo: Lin Cheung

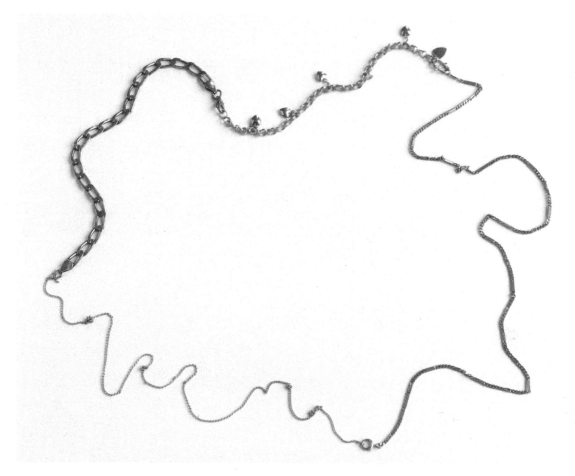

the hospice after relatives had died, had a letter with it, although the opposite was true of most of the other jewellery received.

Mike Guy and Rebecca de Quin were brave enough to cut up gold watches and other precious objects inherited from each of their families. They melted them down to cast their own wedding rings. A leftover piece of the mixed gold was made into a necklace for their young daughter. The rings look quite simple, but the story behind how they came into existence is evocative. By recycling the family gold, they have created symbols of their love and commitment to each other from items which they would have kept, but might never have worn or used. They have made three pieces of very personal jewellery which they will be proud to wear for a long time to come.

Covering or partially covering an existing piece of jewellery is another possible way of recycling it and extending its life. Whilst a student at Middlesex University, Madeleine Furness made a collection of *Lightning-Safe Jewellery*, which is coated with a rubber solution to make it safe to wear in an electrical storm. The original piece remains inside its rubber coating, protecting the wearer from being struck by lightning and itself protected from the wear and tear to which it might normally be exposed. In this way, a precious item is also kept safe from being seen, while still remaining wearable, whereas, if it was locked away in a safe or bank vault, it would be hidden from view and thus unavailable to be worn.

Wedding Rings and Necklace,
Rebecca de Quin, 2006. Mixed
gold items.
Photo: Jim Cheatle

ABOVE *Box of Leftover Gold*,
Rebecca de Quin, 2006.
Photo: Jim Cheatle

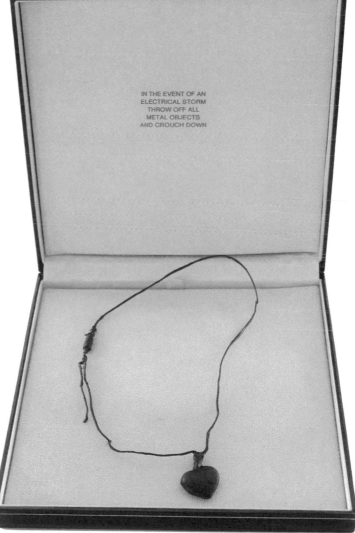

'Lightning Safe' Jewellery – Locket,
Madeleine Furness, 2003. Silver/
base-metal found jewellery, magnets,
synthetic rubber, customised
jewellery box.
Photo: Robin Turner

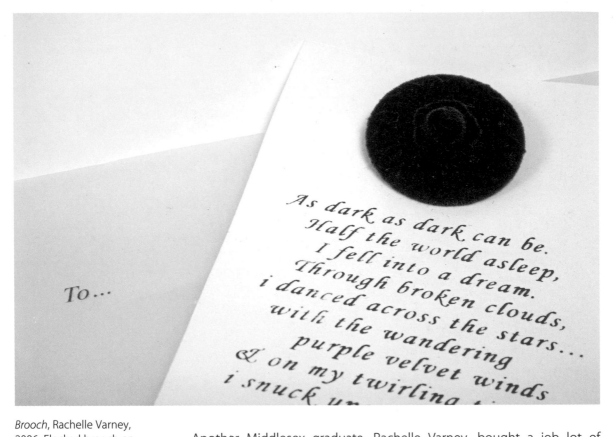

As dark as dark can be.
Half the world asleep,
I fell into a dream.
Through broken clouds,
i danced across the stars...
with the wandering
purple velvet winds
& on my twirling
i snuck un

To...

Brooch, Rachelle Varney, 2006. Flocked brooch on card with poem.
Photo: Anthony Coleman

Another Middlesex graduate, Rachelle Varney, bought a job lot of brooches from a market stall. She covered each of them in a rich, deep, plum-coloured layer of flocking, giving them mysterious shapely contours, merely hinting at what might lie beneath their velvety covering. Packaged with a poem written by her, they take on an intriguing new persona, not only fascinating and desirable, but eminently wearable too.

The French sculptor Jean-Luc Vilmouth employed a similar technique in his multi-coated garden tools of the 1980s, rendering familiar objects barely recognisable when their forms had become enlarged and blurred. Flocking is an industrial coating process, perhaps more readily associated with wallpaper than jewellery. Electrostatically charged fibres are attracted to an adhesive-covered surface, giving the effect of a napped cloth such as suede, velour, baize or velvet.

Buying second-hand jewellery from a market stall or charity shop involves a certain amount of human interaction, even if the seller is not the original owner of the jewellery. Buying jewellery online, however – for instance, on eBay – puts a certain amount of distance between the purchaser and the vendor, although, conversely, they are more likely to be the original owner with an emotional attachment to the object they are selling. Laura Potter

Lifetime Medal 8901815476,
Laura Potter, 2006.
9 ct gold, 18 ct gold,
antique ribbon.
Photo: Laura Potter

endorses this sense of emotional remoteness by engraving the lot number of her eBay purchase on the medals she makes from gold lockets and pendants, both of which are examples of emotionally charged types of jewellery. A cold stark number becomes an almost perverse echo of the engraved name often found on a piece of jewellery, an obvious sign of having belonged to someone. This is rather similar to the way in which people are depersonalised by labelling when they are patients in a hospital, or prison inmates.

German jeweller Barbara Pröpstl has used fabric coverings as a permanent way of revitalising old jewellery. She has made comforting red covers for parts of some of her pieces from old clothes and scraps of fabric. The choice of colour gives the impression that the objects might be receiving medical care from the Red Cross. They are treated with as much love and attention as if they were wounded soldiers. There are also connotations in the way she works of reupholstering a piece of antique furniture.

RIGHT *4 Stick Pins*,
Barbara Pröpstl, 2004.
Brass, 14 ct gold, cloth.
Photo: Barbara Pröpstl

BELOW *2 Stick Pins*,
Barbara Pröpstl, 2004.
Silver, cloth.
Photo: Barbara Pröpstl

Some of the broken jewellery she has 'mended' in this way was given to her by an aunt to reuse, while other pieces are made from jewellery she used to wear, along with flea-market purchases. Pröpstl writes, 'It is hard to part with things that have grown old, they are sleeping in boxes, in upper drawers and in cupboards … Sometimes we take them out and paint them over, envelop them, give them a new look and preserve them …' One series of *Shards* are broken fragments of china protected by yellow felt slings and harnesses, as if to keep them from harm and at the same time, to protect the wearer from their sharp edges.

Shard 3, necklace,
Barbara Pröpstl, 2003.
Porcelain, felt.
Photo: Barbara Pröpstl

Temporary add-on surrounds are Heike Baschta's solution for rejuvenating an old or broken ring. Her luxurious 'fur funnels' are made to enfold and pamper the stone-setting on a ring, as though dressing it up to go out for the evening. A series of colourful felt covers, intended to conceal and disguise broken rings, has a jauntier, more everyday aspect. The same ring could be worn with a felt topping during the day, changing over to fur for evening wear.

There is a certain perversity in the way that some contemporary practitioners are recycling jewellery. Gijs Bakker has produced 'Real', a collection of jewels inspired by and usually incorporating a piece of costume jewellery. Painstaking research goes into making a miniature version of a paste brooch or necklace using real gemstones. Tracking down the right stones, having them cut and set in exactly the same, sometimes outmoded way, combined with having them made by other people, turns an insignificant piece of faux jewellery into a clever, but costly, oeuvre. The idea has the same kitsch appeal as some of American artist Jeff Koons's outrageously over-the-top, but wickedly witty sculpture.

The Heirlooms' New Clothes, Heike Baschta, 1996. Coypu fur, fox fur, old rings. Photo: courtesy of Jewellery Design, Design Department, Düsseldorf University of Applied Sciences, Düsseldorf, Germany.

Rubystick Brooch (one-off),
Gijs Bakker (executed by
Pauline Barendse), 2006.
Seven 3.66 ct dove red
rubies, 14 ct white gold,
palladium, metal, glass.
Photo: Rien Bazen

Ring, white gold, aquamarine
glass, Karl Fritsch, 1995.
Photo: Karl Fritsch

By making additions to old, sometimes broken jewellery, Karl Fritsch recycles in layers. For example, he has taken traditional rings, often set with gemstones, drilled into them, manipulated and cut them up. By casting and recasting them several times over, he arrives at a series of strangely misshapen rings with elongated, twisted, extra parts grafted onto the original, usually conventional, shape. In an unusual and faintly sacrilegious act, some rings have been totally covered with matt black or gold paint. This daring, energetic approach has teased new life out of what started off as fairly standard items of jewellery. In his willingness to tamper with tradition, Fritsch has refashioned them, both physically and conceptually, with a playful exaggeration and plasticity.

Ring, 14k gold, 8k gold,
oxidised, Karl Fritsch, 2003.

Ring, gold, oxidised silver,
diamond, Karl Fritsch, 2006.

Ring, 14k gold, Karl Fritsch,
1993. Photos: Karl Fritsch

Chewing Gum – A Memory,
brooch, Rory Hooper, 2005.
Gold-plated silver, stone.
Photo: Rory Hooper

'In a society which constantly replaces its objects according to varying fashions, the number of "leftover" objects tossed aside is rapidly increasing.' So says Rory Hooper. His radical remedy is to flatten old pieces of jewellery with a hammer and then set them with precious stones, sometimes gold-plating them, to reinvent new jewellery from discarded pieces. This dramatic process, has irrevocably altered treasured family and personal possessions, including a ring made by his father. Not only does it represent a symbolic flattening of the memories held within a piece of old jewellery and a point of no return, but, surprisingly, it also has a positive, cathartic effect of generating fresh possibilities and a new way ahead.

There are many inventive ways of turning old jewellery into new. Just as in nature certain seeds need fire to propagate them, so some jewellers use destructive processes in order to construct something new.

Chewing Gum – A Memory,
ring, Rory Hooper, 2005.
Gold-plated silver, amethyst.
Photo: Rory Hooper

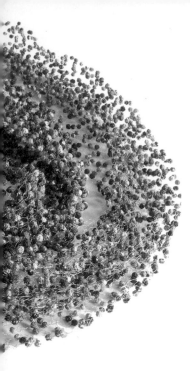

2 Waste Not, Want Not

THIS CHAPTER examines how discarded materials have been used to make jewellery. The generation who lived through the Second World War and the subsequent time of austerity were conditioned never to throw anything away. Growing your own vegetables was a recognised part of the war effort in Britain and the adage 'Waste not, want not' encouraged people to produce a wealth of meals created from potato peelings and other food offcuts which might normally have been discarded. It also spawned inventive clothing, sewn and knitted from deconstructed clothes, coats made from old blankets and blouses made from parachute material, especially during wartime rationing, which continued for several years after the war had ended.

Julie Cook, who initially trained as a nurse and more recently as a jeweller, espouses this tradition by using old bed linen, blankets and other found fabrics to make garments of a quasi-medical or beneficial nature. All these works come with clear instructions as to their use and function, combining an air of seriousness with a tongue-in-cheek humour. They are always white or cream and impeccably made, which gives them an air of purity and inspires confidence in the possibility that wearing them may bring comfort and relief from phobias or other medical conditions.

One collection of Cook's work, *Madness of the Bulls*, was based on research into female bullfighters, of which there have apparently been a significant number. The heroine of *Talk to Her*, a film by the Spanish director Almodóvar, is also a female bullfighter. This series of sewn textile pieces are padded and quilted to protect or give courage to the matador or toreador wearing them before, during or after the fight. Particular areas of the body are clothed for specific reasons. For example, the *Shoes of Suerte* are for luck or destiny, a pair of soft, foot coverings with a cushioned lining, which look a bit like a cross between medieval shoes and a pair of slippers.

The *Bilateral Body Bumpers*, from the same series, are to guard against knocks or blows to the body. Attached to the arms with crossed-over

FACING PAGE
TOP LEFT *Shoes of Suerte*, Julie Cook, 2005. Household linen, with wadding, lining and tapes.

TOP RIGHT *Bilateral Body Bumpers*, Julie Cook, 2005. Cotton pillowcases, blanket pads, with knotted quilting and ties.

BELOW *Zapateado Injured Soles*, Julie Cook, 2006. Calico and hospital blanket with darned toes and button taps. All photos: Julie Cook

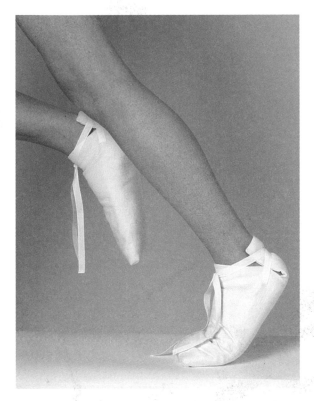

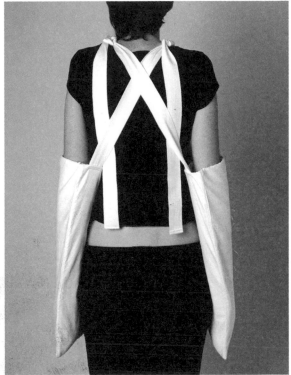

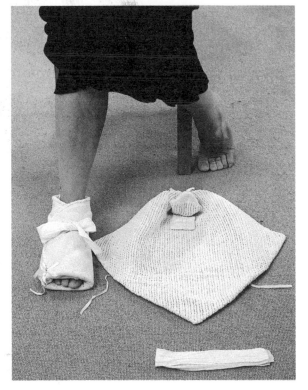

straps, the *Body Bumpers* contain visual references to nurses' uniforms and straitjackets.

Zapateado Injured Soles are made from a folded hospital blanket and are intended to provide affection for the feet and increase the wearer's neuro-sensory perception.

The discarded material that Cook works with comes ready-charged with emotions and stains from the human life cycle. To this she has added several more layers of mythology and utility.

After the Second World War, the next generation grew up with the 'waste not, want not' ethos firmly embedded in their psyche, so perhaps understandably, when more prosperous times came, they rebelled and indulged in the luxury of being able to waste and still not want. Hand-knitting and home cooking were scorned in favour of manufactured goods. This has led to the rise of a supermarket and fast-food culture, where most items are packaged, usually in plastic. There

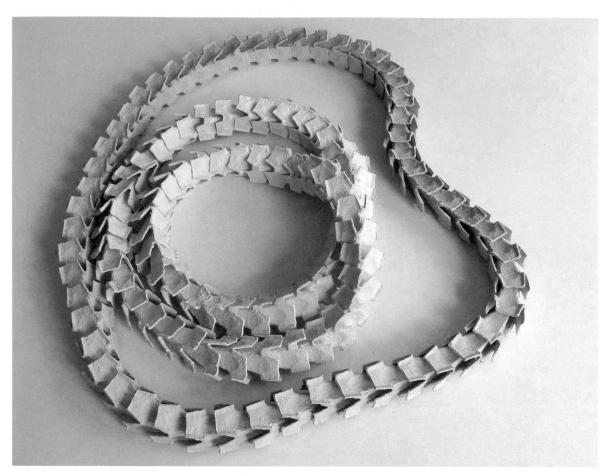

Egg-box Collar, Verena
Sieber-Fuchs, 1992. Egg
boxes, wire.
Photo: Sebastian Sieber

is now growing alarm at the amount of stuff being thrown away each day, but also a growing awareness of the consequences of rubbish being buried in landfill sites and the risks to health and the environment which that exposes us to. However, the situation is gradually starting to change. Britain is beginning to catch up with other European countries in making recycling easier and more accessible. Moreover, our appreciation for things of quality, whether they are handmade, homemade, or utilise the latest computer technology, seems to have come full circle.

Verena Sieber-Fuchs has been working by hand with various discarded materials for many years. Her training in textiles is apparent whether she is working with richly coloured foil chocolate wrappers rolled into tiny beads, or snippets of Super 8 film from the cutting-room floor – all are treated with the same meticulous care and attention to detail. Using fine crochet to join a myriad of small pieces together, she conjures feathery collars out of film and turns sweet papers into sumptuous stoles or swathes of fabric. She has also used pill packets, newspaper, egg cartons and fruit wrappers in her work.

Burnt Collar, Verena Sieber-
Fuchs, 2001. Burnt film, Inox
knitted. Photo: Sebastian Sieber

BELOW *Sprüngli Collar*, Verena
Sieber-Fuchs, 2000. Sprüngli
chocolate wrappers, Inox
crocheted.
Photo: Sebastian Sieber

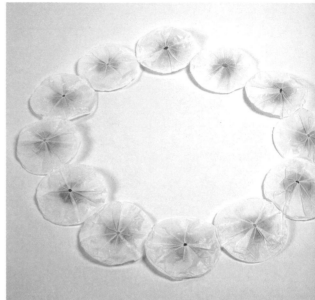

ABOVE LEFT *Squares Neckpiece*
(detail), Claudie Fenwick,
2007. Plastic carrier bags.
Photo: Anthony Coleman

ABOVE RIGHT *Circles Neckpiece*,
Claudie Fenwick, 2007.
Plastic carrier bags.
Photo: Anthony Coleman

Plastic carrier bags must be among the most ubiquitous discarded objects to be seen in either the urban or rural landscape. They lodge in trees and float in streams, choking swans and fish. City foxes eat takeaway suppers from them, and shoppers rarely refuse one at the supermarket checkout. But some exciting jewellery and accessories are being made from this rather unpromising, mundane material. In India, a number of community projects are transforming plastic bags and waste plastic sheeting into stylish bags fit for Western tastes.

Several Middlesex University jewellery students have used plastic bags to great effect in their work. Claudie Fenwick's delicate, pretty necklaces are made from carrier bags. The material is not immediately recognisable, because of the subtle choices she has made in her use of colour, and the clever ruching technique she has employed. The plastic has been worked as though it were a length of finely woven dress fabric. This has been achieved by a very low-tech method: using an electric iron and a sheet of brown paper.

Similarly, Rachel Darbourne, has transformed the common carrier bag into luxurious fluffy necklaces and bracelets reminiscent of Hawaiian lei garlands. They are surprisingly soft to the touch and are sometimes combined with marabou feathers, which gives them a glamorous aspect in contrast with their lowly origins. The method of making them is very labour-intensive, and involves cutting the circles out by hand or stamping them out and then threading them onto nylon fishing wire. Although each individual circle of plastic is quite flimsy on its own, when

ABOVE *Necklace*, Rachel Darbourne, 1996. Plastic bin bags, nylon.
Photo: Anthony Coleman

RIGHT *Bracelet*, Rachel Darbourne, 1996. Plastic bin bags, carrier bags, nylon.
Photo: Anthony Coleman

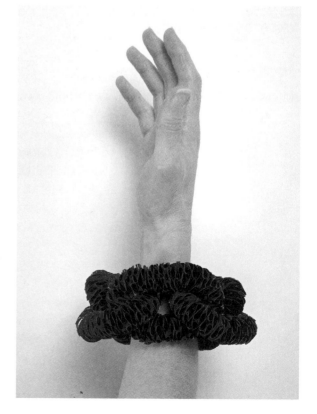

hundreds of them are put together, they make a substantial finished piece.

Kristina Kitchener has used the clear plastic bags that vegetables are packed in at the supermarket to make a long white chain necklace. By twisting and ironing thin strips of the material, then allowing them to curl back on themselves, each link has taken on a different three-dimensional form from the next one. The overall effect is rather frilly and lacy, whereas her chain necklace made from black-plastic refuse sacks has much flatter links. The way in which they have been cut out in layers and ironed to

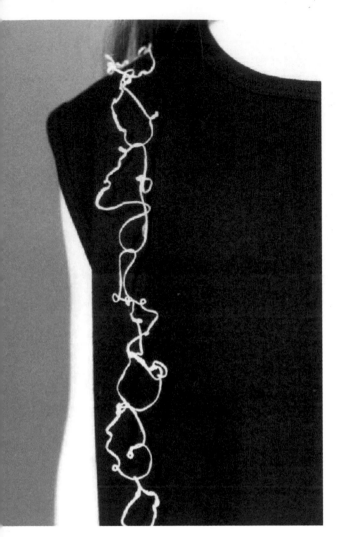

ABOVE *21 links: A chain of events*, Kristina Kitchener, 2007. Black-plastic refuse sacks.
Photo: Emma Palmer

LEFT *White Chain Necklace*, Kristina Kitchener, 2003. Clear plastic vegetable bags.
Photo: Kristina Kitchener

FACING PAGE *Ring*, Sarah Pritchard, 2006. Plastic drinks bottle, plastic tubing.
Photo: Anthony Coleman

fuse them has resulted in oddly shaped links, which look more like forged, blackened steel than plastic.

Kitchener has also worked in a similar way with plastic milk containers to make chains, using a domestic iron to flatten strips of the material and a soldering iron to seal and join the links. Sarah Pritchard has gone to some lengths to disguise the humble provenance of her bracelets and rings made from plastic milk containers and drinks bottles. Some are decorated with pyrographically cut patterns, which fit in very well with the translucent material. Although the surfaces have been worked on, some of the rings still retain their bottle shapes, giving them a humorous aspect. The edges are finished with coloured plastic tubing, which has a multi-functional purpose in that it brings colour to each piece, defines the edges and makes each one smoother and more comfortable to wear.

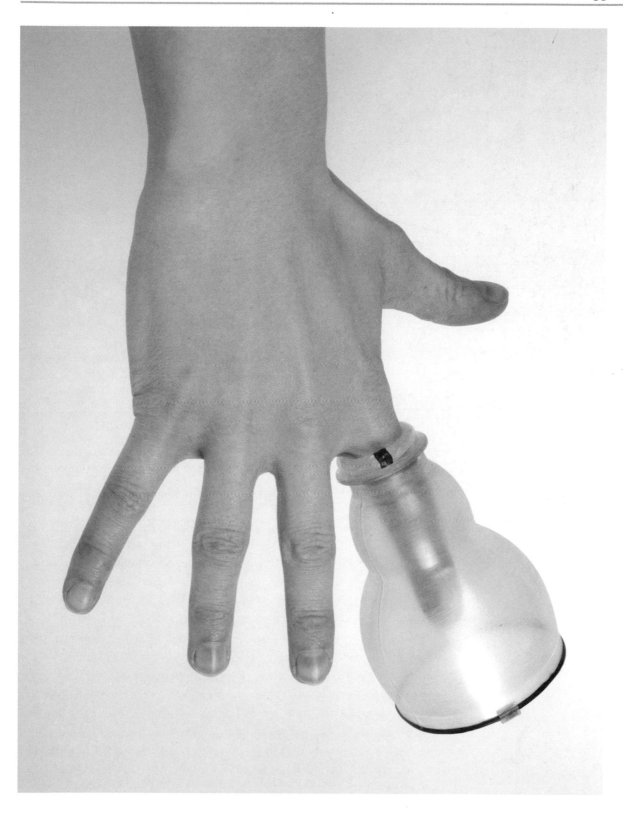

ABOVE LEFT *Brooch*,
Pavel Opočenský, 1997.
Bakelite, 8 x 8 x 1 cm.
Photo: Martin Tuma

ABOVE RIGHT *Ski Brooch*,
Pavel Opočenský, 1998.
Old skis, wood, polyurethane,
steel, fibre glass, 8.4 x 7.4 x
1.2 cm.
Photo: Martin Tuma

In his collection of jewellery, *Bakelitomania*, Pavel Opočenský made exquisite brooches from fragments of industrial Bakelite, typically, electrical box covers found in disused factories in the former Czechoslovakia. They have hardly been changed from their original state, except to decide which parts to use and which to leave out. Every piece retains a carefully selected reminder of its former use – for instance, the words '500 volts', or a tiny perforated area – which becomes the focal point of each brooch. The brooches have a dark brooding presence both in colour and material, embodying more than an echo of a previous industrial era and of the history of this early form of plastic. Pursuing a similar train of thought, Opočenský next made a series of brooches from old skis. Taking the opportunity of carving into the layers of different materials which make up the structure of the ski, he has created multicoloured, small-scale reliefs, which have a painterly quality.

Paper and cardboard – in the form of fast-food boxes, coffee cups, leaflets and newspapers – have become an all too familiar sight littering the streets and countryside. They may not seem to have an immediate connection with jewellery – exotic handmade papers might spring to mind more readily – but there is a strong tradition of using these discarded materials for making jewellery. In the early 1980s, Willem Honing used brown paper and string to make cylindrical ruffle necklaces, and Annelies Planteydt, now better known for her forged gold jewellery, made bracelets and necklaces from slices of plain, unadorned cardboard. More recently, while a student at Middlesex University, Leonie Philpot made long garlands

Garland (detail), Leonie
Philpot, 2006. Corrugated
cardboard, gold-plated
earring hooks.
Photo: Leonie Philpot

from spiralled, corrugated cardboard. The only decorative element is the
way in which the material has been bent to make it curve, exposing the
honeycombed edges to view.

In one sense the daily newspaper is the epitome of ephemera: the contents
are out of date by the end of the day when tomorrow's paper is already being
prepared and printed. On the other hand, the physical substance of
newspaper takes a long time to break down, even when it is exposed to the
weather. Julian Robinson's *Spit Ring* is made from a found copy of the *Financial
Times* and saliva. In the catalogue from the Heirlooms exhibition, where
members of the Association for Contemporary Jewellers were asked to
consider what archaeologists will be digging up and discovering in a
thousand years' time, and to make jewellery in response, Robinson describes
the piece wittily as 'an ecologically sound gold ring (hallmark pending)'.

While abandoned newspapers are often still a visible presence until
someone clears them up, other forms of paper live a far more discreet life.
What happens, for instance, to disused bank notes? Not much is heard
about them outside infamous events such as the Great Train Robbery in
1960s Britain, when a vast amount of them were stolen. Deborah Zeldin-

O'Neill combined them with polycarbonate to make *Banknote Knuckleduster*, a ring spanning four fingers of one hand, also for the Heirlooms exhibition.

Rumour has it that vinyl records are making a comeback, so will some of us rue the day that we decided to recycle them? Ariane Hartman makes rings cut from old records. Keeping a fragment of the song title visible sends a message, perhaps giving it a new meaning, or sending us on a nostalgic trip down memory lane. Philipp Eberle, on the other hand, cuts circles out of old records, domes them up and welds them together using heat, in the process completely transforming the flat discs into hollow spheres. Old records become the new jet in these necklaces of lustrous, black beads. Eberle says that 'Waste scientists call this procedure "upcycling", giving waste back its worth'.

Pearl Necklace, Philipp Eberle, 2006. Vinyl record.
Photo: Philipp Eberle

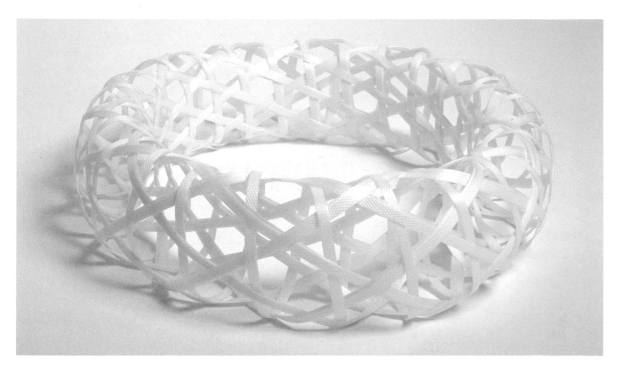

White Collar, Peiling Lee,
1998. Parcel binding.
Photo: Anthony Coleman

Plastic parcel strapping is another common form of everyday litter. An extremely strong woven material, it is used to secure packages tightly under tension. For this reason, it does not break or biodegrade easily and can be a real hazard underfoot. Attracted by the colours and availability of the material, Peiling Lee has used it by weaving long strips of the material together to make bold, intricately worked cylindrical collars. Although it is carefully put together, her white neckpiece has an appealingly random, criss-cross, lattice-work look about it.

Blue Collar, Peiling Lee, 1998.
Parcel binding.
Photo: Anthony Coleman

A blue collar made out of the same material is woven more tightly into pod shapes. This method of construction gives the necklace an elastic quality so that it can be stretched enough to be put on over the head.

Basket-maker Lois Walpole has used a variety of discarded materials including parcel binding and juice cartons from an early stage of her career to make groundbreaking work. By handling these materials inventively and exploiting their innate texture and colour, she has made handsome laundry baskets and fashionable bags and has also broadened the scope of basketry in an inspirational way.

Tectan® is the trade name for a recycled material manufactured from compressed juice cartons. It is made in panels and looks similar to cork, but contains flecks of colour with flashes of silver from the inner lining of the Tetra Paks. Trays and place mats are made from it at present, but it could also be an interesting material from which to make jewellery.

Laundry Basket,
Lois Walpole, 1995. Juice
cartons, 90 x 79 x 35 cm.
Photo: Lois Walpole

Offcuts of all kinds, including wood, paper and rubber, are the sorts of
materials which Pierre Degen salvages for making jewellery and other
objects. He often works in an intuitive way, laying out a number of bits and
pieces and working directly with the materials on the body. Without having
a preconceived idea of how the piece will turn out, it is only when the parts

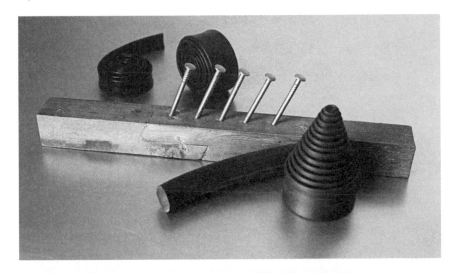

Materials for Handpiece,
Pierre Degen, 1994.
Photo: Charley Whitehorn

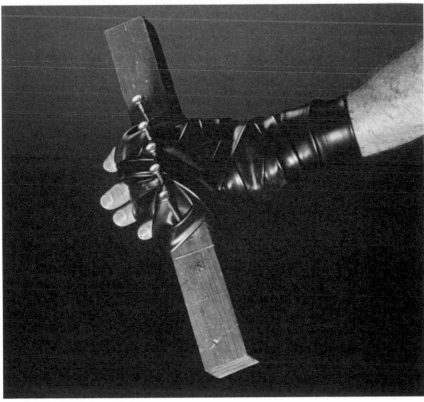

Handpiece, Pierre Degen,
1994. Wood, nails, rubber
inner tube.
Photo: Charley Whitehorn

Materials for Armpiece,
Pierre Degen, 1994.
Photo: Charley Whitehorn

FACING PAGE *Armpiece,*
Pierre Degen, 1994. Wood
offcuts, rubber inner tube.
Photo: Charley Whitehorn

are assembled on the body that they become a piece of jewellery, which lends an element of surprise and sometimes humour. Many of these pieces are joined together or articulated with elastic bands or rubber inner tubes from tyres. Disparate objects and materials, often quite ordinary and commonplace, take on an extraordinary new dimension because they are put together with great care and precision; yet the end result looks lively and spontaneous, as though the various component parts might have been randomly thrown together.

These examples bear witness to the many ways in which abandoned materials, which may look quite unpromising to some, can be made into jewellery and accessories. It seems that intervention can be minimal, and materials do not always need to undergo a total transformation to take on a new persona; they just require handling with sensitivity and an awareness of their inherent properties. A piece of jewellery can be equally interesting and unusual if the recycled elements are easily identifiable, depending on how inventively the materials are used and put together.

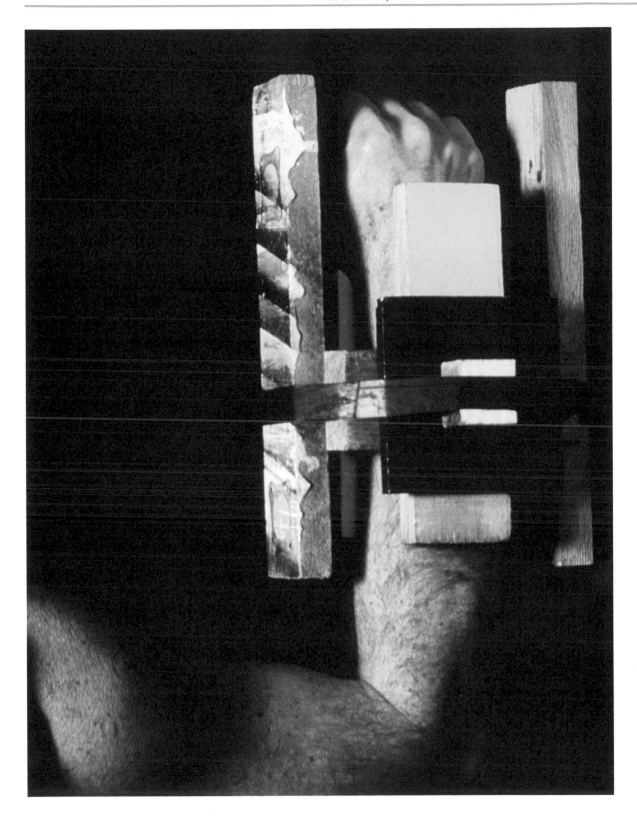

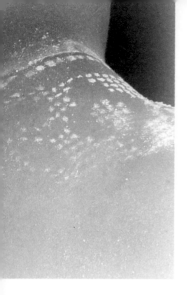

3 Ephemeral Jewellery:
Something and nothing

THIS CHAPTER looks at a genre of jewellery which gets top marks in the sustainability stakes, requiring next to no physical materials to make. Using marks on the skin, dust, light, or images projected onto the body, a photograph or performance can often be the finished work. Like the emperor's new clothes, it could be thought of as non-jewellery or negative jewellery, but the concept behind it is positive enough. The ecological downside is that this kind of jewellery often relies on photography or film for lasting documentation, which of course may involve the use of environmentally damaging chemicals in processing the images.

In 1973, Gijs Bakker made *Schaduwsieraad*, which literally translates from Dutch as *Shadow Jewellery*. Metal bands were fastened round various parts of the body, which on removal left a pronounced indentation in the skin – just as the elasticated ribbing on a sock might leave a mark around the lower leg, or a glance in the mirror, on waking, often reveals the creases of the sheets or pyjama seams imprinted on the skin.

Marks could be made on the body with an object made especially for the purpose, or something fairly anonymous like a rubber band, either of which might become part of the final piece. On the other hand, the mark-making object could be discarded to allow an image of the marks to take centre stage as the finished work.

This way of working seems to have its roots in ancient tribal rituals such as African scarification, where patterns are cut into the skin, or tattooing, traditionally used by the New Zealand Maoris and other Pacific-based tribal groups as a permanent way of inking patterns onto the skin. Tattooing used to be a body decoration particularly associated with sailors and later with motorbike-riding Hell's Angels, or followers of Heavy Metal music. More recently, it has become an increasingly popular fashion statement, one which crosses different areas of society, transcending cults, age and gender groups on a global scale. However, both scarification and tattooing are

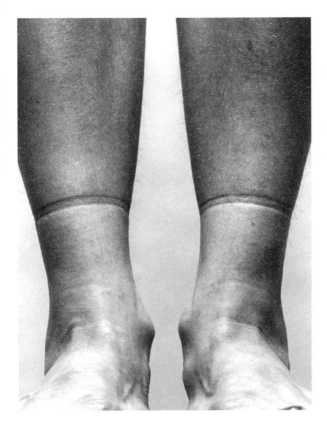

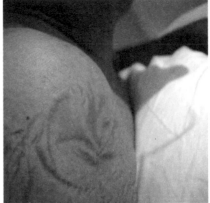

ABOVE *Pillow Marks*, Philipp Eberle, 2003. Photo: Philipp Eberle

LEFT *Shadow Jewellery – Legs*, Gijs Bakker, 1973. Photo: Ton Baadenhuysen

BELOW *Lightweight*, Warwick Freeman, 2001. Colour slide, Photo: Ton Werkhoven

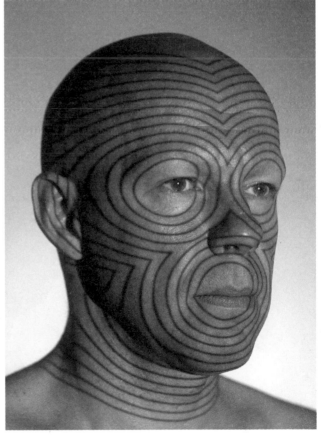

permanent ways of marking the skin, whereas the work discussed in this chapter is transient, but, like the traditional Indian way of patterning the hands with henna, can produce a similar visual effect.

The mask made by New Zealand jeweller Warwick Freeman for the exhibition *Maskerade*, held at Galerie Ra, Amsterdam in 2001, looks like a tattoo, but is actually made by projecting a slide onto the face and head. In the exhibition catalogue, Freeman writes, 'A full-face tattoo has enormous cultural weight. My mask is made of light'. Within the piece and the statement about it, he plays with the idea of tattooing both verbally and visually, using the minimal means of a slide and a projector. Once an image of the projection has been obtained, that is the finished piece.

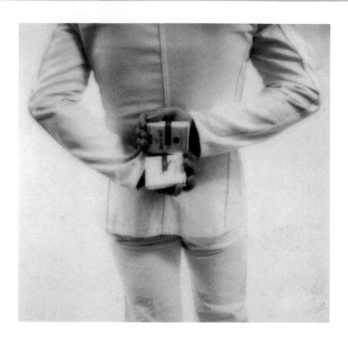

Everyday Adornment,
Robert Smit, 1975. Polaroid
sx70 photograph.
Photo: Robert Smit

In the mid-1970s, Robert Smit made a series of Polaroid photographs of himself simply holding two cigarette packets against his body in various ways. Called *Everyday Adornment*, the results were an intriguing mixture of a performance work and the relationship of body to object. This suggested that any object could be jewellery if it was put forward as such, which was a radical way for a jeweller to work at the time.

More recently, Gisbert Stach embedded a ring of flints into the heels of a pair of shoes, in order to make sparks fly when he walked. *Firestep* was made in 1994 using 18 ct gold wire. In *1000 Rings*, published by Lark Books, Stach writes that 'On his way he leaves a practically imperceptible golden trace'. He has also embedded gold jewellery into a tarmac road, to be walked or driven over.

In recent work by Claire Jeffs, jewellery is conjured from urban situations, with the help of photography. While out walking, she identifies and photographs a variety of objects in the landscape as potential jewellery. By collaging herself into the photograph, carefully positioned in relation to particular buildings, these objects become diamond rings, hair ornaments or earrings. Jeffs refers to them as a series of 'sketches', and in each of them the shadowy silhouette of a figure dominates the foreground of the photograph. In one sketch, a decorative swag on the front of an old building becomes a spiral gold earring. In another, the silhouette stands with arm outstretched and hand extended, so that the diamond image from a shop sign perches neatly on an outstretched finger.

Find from an Urban Jewellery Expedition, Claire Jeffs, 2007. Gold spiral-twist earring.
Photo: Claire Jeffs

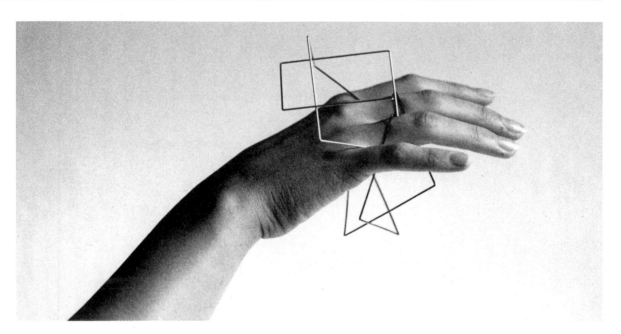

Armbands by Charles Marks,
1982. Steel.
Photographed as rings by
Manfred Nisslmüller, 1987

Jeffs' work has developed from previous conceptual, performative jewellery, often taking place in public spaces, where, for instance, a hand might be placed between railings and the photograph of the activity becomes the final piece. It would appear to be quite a sustainable way of making jewellery, the journey is made on foot, and only elements in the immediate surroundings are used, with nothing being taking away other than a photographic image. Of course, this does not take into account the mode of travel to and from the walk, or the means by which the resulting images were generated.

By appropriating or borrowing other jewellers' work, Manfred Nisslmüller made new pieces of work. Without altering them physically, he photographed them worn on a different part of the body than the one they were originally intended for. In this way, a neckpiece becomes an arm-piece, minimal steel armbands become giant rings, and a brooch becomes an earpiece.

In *Pocket Recorder*, made over a period of nine years, 1984–93, Nisslmüller replaced jewellery with sound. Where a brooch might have been worn on the body, the tape recorder repeated the word 'brooch' over and over again in a continuous chant, until it became in his words 'irritating – therefore disturbing' thus backing up his thesis that 'disturbance is jewellery', one of the texts he carved into the walls of the V&V jewellery gallery in Vienna in 1985.

In ephemeral work, there is often a play on positive and negative as in forensic science, where surfaces might be dusted with a fine powder, or a detailed impression of a culprit's fingerprints may be captured on transparent, sticky tape, thereby turning the negative back into a positive again. When artist Christine Borland was shortlisted for the Turner Prize in 1997, the film made about her art at the time showed her working on *After a true story – Giant and Fairy Tales*, using the shapes defined by the large replicated bones of a giant and the tiny bones of a dwarf which were placed on glass shelves and dusted over. The art was the image, or lack of it, left in the dust when the bones were removed. Those traces, memories of two tragic lives, could be viewed through the glass from underneath, giving the work another perspective.

An interest in the way dust collects informs Linsey Bell's elegiac, lyrical jewellery. The human body sloughs off dead skin and loose hairs during every minute of its living existence. Her black and white *Dust Interaction* photographs of 2004, required only a strong light source to show up the fine particles of dust coming from the body, and a camera to capture and

Dust Interaction 1,
Linsey Bell, 2004. Black and white photograph.
Photo: Linsey Bell

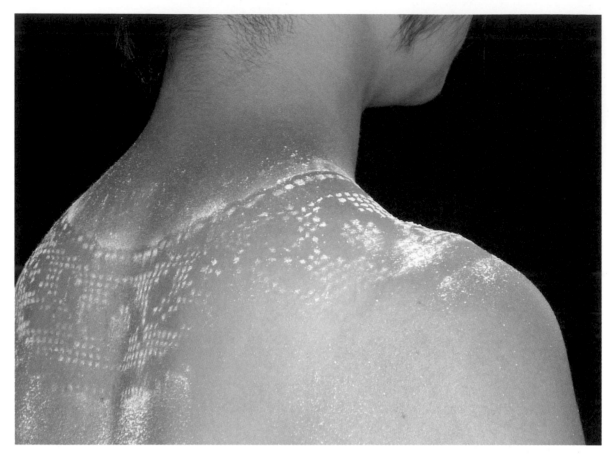

Lace Collar, Millie Cullivan,
2004. Talc.
Photo: Caroline Broadhead

fix the image for posterity. The simplicity of these shots belies the careful thought and preparation which went into making them and the determination to realise ideas at a sophisticated level.

A related line of thought can be seen in Millie Cullivan's *Lace Collar* from 2004. It is a neckpiece made by sieving white powder through the minute holes in a piece of lace, much as you might sieve icing sugar onto a cake, thereby filtering a negative pattern of the intricate fabric directly onto the skin. As in Linsey Bell's photographs, it is instructive to imagine the preparatory work that must have preceded the actual moment of taking the pictures. No glue or fixing agent had been applied to the skin beforehand, so any unexpected air or body movement could have been disastrous.

Artist Mona Hatoum's + *and* − motorised sculpture, from 1994, personifies the idea of something and nothing. A double-ended blade revolves horizontally in a box of fine sand; as one half of the blade combs the sand, the other half wipes the marks away, leaving the sand blank, ready to be marked again in a never-ending cycle.

Dress with Holes,
Caroline Broadhead, 1998.
Silk, paint, light, approx. 120
x 60 x 60 cm.
Photo: Noel Brown

Light is the medium needed by traditional jewellery to be seen at its best. Caroline Broadhead has used sunlight, as well as electric light, for some of her many installations. She has also worked extensively with light and shadow. These are captured and made manifest using the shadow cast by a suspended garment. Typically, Broadhead makes these dresses out of a translucent material such as net or silk, and the shadow is given a physical presence by being drawn in paint or pencil on the wall behind the dress. In this way Broadhead plays with transience and permanence, a fleeting shadow being a permanent fixture solely for the duration of the exhibition. There is a subtle shift in balance as the shadow becomes more substantial than the form itself.

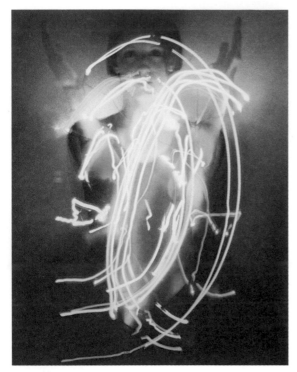

Line of Light, Georgina
Edwards, 2002. Strip light.
Photo: Trefor Ball

Candlelight has been used as a major element in some of artist Christian Boltanski's installations. The flickering light distorts the shadows of suspended flat metal figures and projects them onto the wall behind. The heat from the candles keeps both figures and shadows moving in an eerie, contorted dance, creating a powerful, ghostly atmosphere.

In the 1920s, artist and photographer Man Ray invented what he called 'rayographs' by exposing photographic paper with composed objects on it to any light source – even sunlight. Artist Chris Wainwright made swirling photographic drawings with light at night in the 1980s. A decade later artist Donald Urquhart made a series of drawings by leaving natural objects on paper in daylight over a period of time. The yellowing of the paper caused by exposure to the sun produced a negative image.

While a student at Middlesex University, Georgina Edwards made *Line of Light* encompassing the whole body with trails of coloured light, made from swinging a strip light around the body and capturing it on camera. Effectively, this is a way of drawing with light, much as one might draw in the dark with a lit sparkler or a lighted torch.

To make a mask for *Maskerade*, I took pictures of my face 'masked' by my hands in various ways. This was interesting in itself, as not only was I having to guess what I would have seen if I had been looking through the viewfinder of the camera, I was also covering my eyes with my hands, thereby rendering myself doubly blind. The colour photographs were processed, photocopied in black and white and then photocopied onto coloured acetate. Looking through the printed acetate, it became possible to see through the places which had previously been obscured by my hands while taking the photographs, as these had become the most transparent and revealing parts of the image.

Ghostings, an installation of mine at m2 Gallery, used translucent and transparent objects suspended over a glass shelf with an overhead light source. Shadows moved about within the metre-square gallery space in such a way that, viewed from a distance, it looked as though there was nothing in the gallery. Closer inspection revealed the elongated shapes of indefinable objects moving about the space in an ambient air current.

FACING PAGE *One-Hand Mask*,
Julia Manheim, 2001.
Photocopy on acetate, elastic.
Photo: Ton Werkhoven

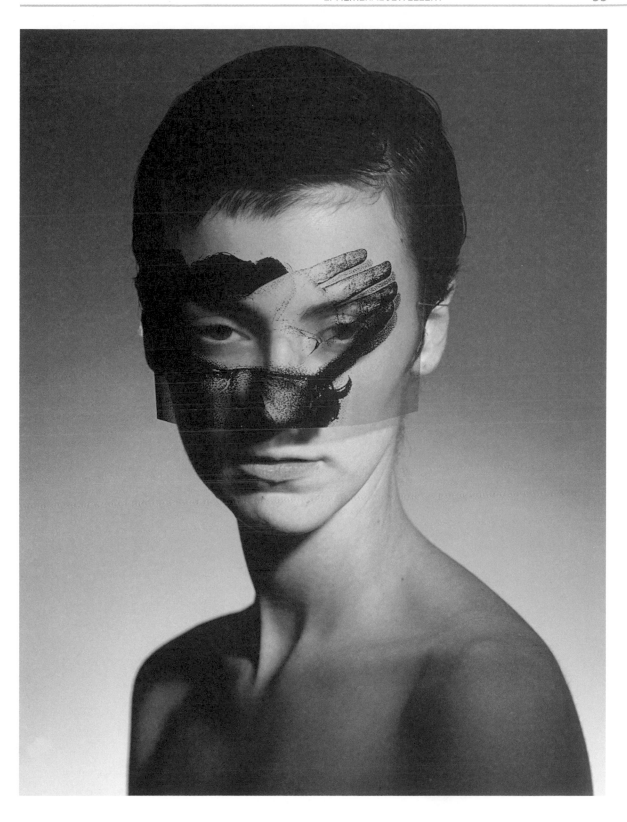

Lenticular 1: Shoulder Lens, Naomi Filmer, 2007. Animated integral image, produced by Create 3D and BluLoop.
Photo: BluLoop

Naomi Filmer works with the body in an ephemeral way that makes her work hard to categorise. She seems to scan and map the body using various techniques in her desire to explore it. For example, in the past she has made silver jewellery from negative spaces between certain parts of the body, such as toes and fingers. Her recent lenticular pieces celebrate regions such as the shoulder or the elbow, by magnifying them so as to bring them to our notice.

As an extension of this work, she has also made short videos of everyday human gestures, or the sound of breathing or coughing. By isolating, amplifying and repeating sounds or movements over and over, the ordinary becomes extraordinary.

As a jewellery student at Middlesex University, Eleni Bagaki's work began by deconstructing old clothes to make jewellery, which led her to focus on exploring the boundaries between clothing and jewellery. This involved projecting images of clothes, which she made from translucent materials, onto her own body. *Beyond My Clothes* produces a fascinating, yet elusive, distorted image of a slender figure trapped inside floating clothing that is much too large for it. It is reminiscent of the Talking Heads film *Stop Making Sense* (1984), where the singer, David Byrne, performs in a massively oversized suit which looks very funny on his slim body.

Writing on your hand with a biro must be a fairly universal way of remembering something important. It will probably not have been as exquisitely written as the calligraphy in Peter Greenaway's film *Pillow Book* from 1996, where chapters of a book are written on a woman's body by her lovers, but apart from serving a practical purpose it could be just the sort of everyday action which sparks off a creative possibility. For example, we are used to seeing rubber stamps in use at a bank or post office and in many other official situations. Sometimes they are used to

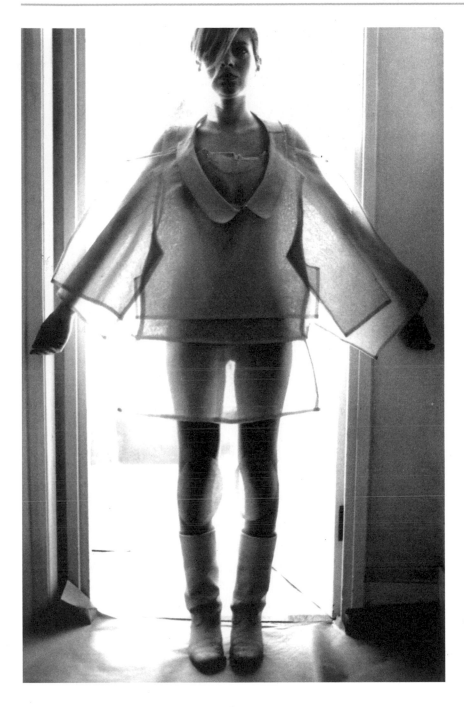

Beyond My Clothes,
Eleni Bagaki, 2004.
Projection: Black and white
photograph.
Photo: Eleni Bagaki

mark the back of the hand on entry to a club or exhibition. Designers
Azumi and David have taken this a step further with their *Rubber Stamp*.
It can be worn as a pendant in its own right, or used to ink the outlines of
archetypal Victorian jewellery onto the skin, rather like a genteel, transient
version of a tattoo.

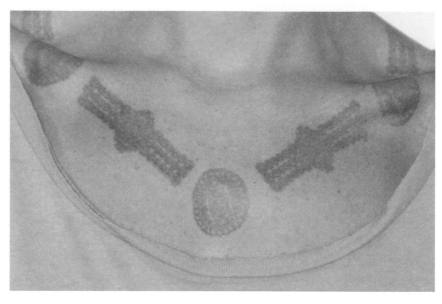

RIGHT *Body Stamp*,
Spring/Summer Collection,
Azumi and David (A'N'D)
2007. Ink.
Photo: Azumi P. Yamashita and
David W. Percival

BELOW *Body Stamp*,
Spring/Summer Collection,
Azumi and David (A'N'D)
2007. Rubber, acrylic, wood,
leather.
Photo: Azumi P. Yamashita and
David W. Percival

Making marks on the skin with metal or ink which will gradually fade and images made from dust or projected light, all seem to be fairly sustainable ways of working. But these examples would be nothing without an image to record them, as on the whole the image is all that remains after the event. Jewellery of this kind can be something in an image or as a memory, but it might be nothing without it. However, no matter how unassuming the original pieces may be, the methods used to make the images are not so sustainable. Although digital photography avoids the serious issues surrounding the ecological disposal of used photographic materials, it does involve using electricity to run computers and to charge up batteries. Printers also require inks, which often come in cartridges that cannot be refilled and are difficult to recycle.

4 Found Objects:
Odds and ends

PEOPLE OFTEN HAVE a fascination with collecting things; indeed such obsessions have at times been the basis for the creation of a major museum or collection. This magpie syndrome usually comes about intentionally, because objects like packaging, postcards, stamps and ornaments have such a strong visual appeal. But sometimes it happens by default, as odds and ends just seem to mount up in the corner of a drawer, or in a jam-jar somewhere. Hans Stofer's *Odds and Sods* pendants in a dog-eared cardboard box are the perfect illustration of this – a mixture of cup hooks, scraps of precious materials and old screws – except that everything in this box has been played with or combined with another item to make some kind of pendant. Each pendant is sold by weight, just as gold is priced per gram. This allows the customer to select and purchase something that fits

Odds and Sods, pendants, Hans Stofer, 2006. Mixed media (comes with a ball chain).
Photo: Hans Stofer

their budget, though it does not guarantee that the value of the materials equals the weight value; thus a piece made out of a nail may turn out to be more expensive than a small piece in gold, plastic or enamel.

Artists and designers tend to like to collect things and have them around in a place where they can see them, so that they might provide food for thought and visual stimulation, in much the same way as objects arranged in a still-life format have provided subject matter for painters since the 17th century. Memento mori portraits from that time included objects such as skulls or hour-glasses as a reminder of the certainty of death, while the Vanitas painting focused on objects which give pleasure, such as musical instruments and wine, reminding the viewer of the worthlessness of worldly goods. Perhaps our collections perform a similar function. Miró, Picasso and other 20th-century artists used found objects in their assemblages and sculpture, and American artist Joseph Cornell incorporated them in his eclectic boxes. Alison Milner's book *Inspirational Objects* consists entirely of an array of objects, simply positioned and photographed, which somehow pander to our instinct for collecting and are a visual reminder of why we do it.

In the 18th century, a tiny scrap of ribbon, thread or metal was sometimes the only memento the mother of an abandoned baby could find to leave with her child. A display of these pitiful, yet poignant items, from babies taken in and cared for at Thomas Coram's Foundling Hospital, can be seen at the Foundling Museum in London.

Button boxes, those treasure troves of buttons of all shapes and sizes, collected by someone else, can sometimes be found in charity shops or car-boot sales. Buttons can be extraordinarily varied and inventive in their own right, made using a variety of techniques (embroidered, cast, carved) from a multitude of different materials including fabric, plastic, bone, shell, metal and horn. Although some people have a phobia about buttons (known as koumpounophobia), more often than not people are fascinated by them. The Pearly Kings and Queens of London are named for their traditional costumes, where entire outfits, including hats, are covered in bold patterns made from the hundreds of iridescent mother-of-pearl buttons sewn onto them.

Pearly King and Queen ensemble, front view: 20th century. Copyright: Museum of London

Kimble Brooches,
Nadia El-Sabei, 2006.
Found buttons, silver.
Photo: Aaron Tilley

There are others who have discovered innovative ways of using buttons to make jewellery, including several Middlesex Jewellery students. Graduate Nadia El-Sabei, for example, grew up between the Middle East and Britain and began collecting found objects from an early age, as they possessed tangible memories of the places she considered to be part of her identity. Her minimal *Kimble Brooches* employ a strictly defined silver bar which holds a button in place and also functions as the means of fastening it to the clothing. The button provides the brooch's colour and decoration. The bar is a silver version of the nylon kimble, the device which shops use to fix the price tag onto a garment so that it cannot easily be removed. In this case, it is there to keep a found button safe and ensure that it does not get lost again.

Emma Palmer encases old buttons in long cylindrical chains of French knitting to make jewellery. The necklaces form a curvaceous mesh around the shape of the buttons, providing glimpses of their colour and the material they are made from. The button collection was started by her great grandmother and was passed down the generations until Palmer's mother gave it to her.

Nicola Williams has found some unusually carved and coloured old buttons to make into simple, silver rings. She has treated the buttons as though they were rounded, unfaceted stones and set them accordingly into classic, cabochon rub-over settings.

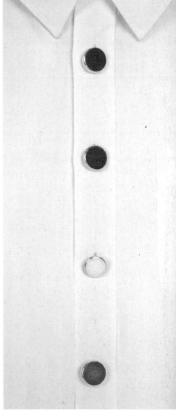

Button Rings, Nicola Williams, 2007. Found buttons, silver.
Photo: Anthony Coleman

ABOVE *Gold Necklace*, Emma Palmer, 2008. Antique buttons, crochet thread.
Photo: Model: Zoe, courtesy nevs model agency

LEFT *Necklace* (detail), Emma Palmer, 2007. Antique buttons, crochet thread.
Photo: Emma Palmer

Roadkill is the gruesome name that Laura Potter has given to an ongoing series of jewellery she makes from anonymous objects found flattened in the road. They are usually made of metal, and in most cases are so mangled when she picks them up that she is unable to identify either their origin or purpose. She refers to them as 'urban flotsam and jetsam washed up in the gutters of my unnatural environment. The work has anecdotal roots: when I was young my father drove over his wedding ring on our driveway. I have no memories of this ring on his finger, only that it used to sit on his dressing table looking squashed and forlorn'.

Roadkill (group), Laura Potter,
2006. Found metal objects,
24 ct gold, 9 ct gold,
pendant 32mm long,
rectangular brooch 62mm
long, wire brooch 55 x 36mm.
Photo: Laura Potter

FACING PAGE *Book Neckpiece*, Mahta Rezvani, 2005. Found hardback book
Photo: Mahta Rezvani

BELOW LEFT *Worn Literature*, necklace, Mahta Rezvani, 2005. Second-hand book, leather.
Photo: Mahta Rezvani

BELOW RIGHT *Ketabdast Armband*, Mahta Rezvani, 2005. Second-hand hardback book.
Photo: Mahta Rezvani

Unwanted books and out-of-date directories become elegant necklaces and bracelets when they are cut up and manipulated by Mahta Rezvani. She has perfected ways of doing this so that the pages stay together and the offcuts can also be made into jewellery. By cutting and twisting a telephone directory or the Yellow Pages, both of which are quite bulky and unwieldy in their original state, she lends them a rhythmical patterned elegance. Edges become more pronounced and important, in contrast to the directory's previous identity, where the information contained within was the most important thing about it.

Richard Wentworth has used books on many occasions in his sculpture and installations. A particular work from 1995 comes to mind: *False Ceiling* consisted of a plethora of books suspended from the ceiling of the Lisson Gallery on steel cables. It was a clever take on the usually completely avisual nature of the suspended ceiling, at the same time as being a vast, impressive umbrella of open flying books to gaze up at and walk beneath.

Another Rose, brooch,
Roseanne Bartley, 2006.
Crushed tin lid, sterling silver,
stainless steel, paint.
Photo: Terence Bogue

Rosette, brooch, Roseanne
Bartley, 2006. Tin lid, sterling
silver, stainless steel, paint.
Photo: Terence Bogue

Found Out – Floral Brooches,
Roseanne Bartley, 2004.
Aluminium ring pulls,
stainless steel, sterling silver.
Photo: Terence Bogue

'My work is a form of surface archaeology. From the mass of detritus and the markings of time and place, traces of culture and environment subtly emerge.' This is what Roseanne Bartley says about *World*, her collection of brooches made from ring pulls from drinks cans and other found objects. Subtly coloured floral brooches are coaxed from old, weathered tin lids, their sharp edges softened to the touch by the paint which transforms them.

Ornaments and crockery have often been used, or have influenced, artists working within various art and design disciplines. In the 1980s, the artist and now film director Julian Schnabel made massive paintings on rows of china plates. Hans Stofer's fruit bowls and dishes are made from shards of broken crockery connected and pieced together with wire, creating a visual effect similar to an exploded diagram of a car engine or the instructions for assembling a piece of flat-pack furniture. In other works, smashed dessert bowls have been reassembled with prominent silicone seams to make larger bowls which have a crazily haphazard look about them.

The same material can also be used to make jewellery. Linsey Bell has cut up some archetypal English ceramic seaside souvenirs and made bracelets from the slices. She refers to these ornaments as 'objects for collecting dust'. The work is made with a humour that has a sly dig at objects many people would regard as highly desirable, but which others might think of as tasteless or kitsch.

Blue Bangle Set, Linsey Bell, 2004. Ceramic.
Photo: William Ireland

Hans Stofer has also used a variety of found objects to make jewellery, as in *Number One*, a ring made from steel and a ping-pong ball, which proudly broadcasts its number-one status in prominent black letters. In this context, the ball takes on a precious quality, tinged with irony now that it is held fast and can never bounce again.

An old box which used to contain a piece of jewellery, where the worn velvet often retains the impression of the brooch or necklace it once contained, is the starting point for Maria Militsi's

Number One, ring, Hans Stofer, 2000. Varnished steel, ping-pong ball.
Photo: Hans Stofer

work. She imagines what might have been in the box and makes a new piece to fit it. This is conjured up from tiny clues, a mixture of detective work and imagination. In *Ciro of Bond Street*, from 2006, she has made a rusty tin bearing the Ciro company logo. It has been fitted into an original satin-lined Ciro jewel box and incorporated into the piece. With the addition of a string of sea pearls (Ciro Pearls Ltd. have been established since 1917), the impetus for the idea and its physical realisation as a wearable necklace become one.

Finding a long, oval, worn leather case with a metal clasp and hinges provided the impetus for Militsi's *Lady's Knife Case*, also made in 2006. The way the purse snaps open gives it the look of the jaws of a baby alligator

Lady's Knife Case, handpiece, Maria Militsi, 2006. Found case, silver, leather.
Photo: Maria Militsi

Ciro of Bond Street, necklace, Maria Militsi, 2006. Found case, steel, sea pearls.
Photo: Maria Militsi

Greetings from...!, necklace, Tina Echterhölter, 2007. Stamp, glass tile, chiffon ribbon, silver chain.
Photo: Tina Echterhölter

when viewed from the side. The little hinged silver handpiece is made to fit the length of the case, lending it the humorous, yet slightly menacing look of a silver tongue being poked out from between the open leather jaws.

Tina Echterhölter has made a series of necklaces called *Greetings from…!* using some of the stamps from letters and postcards sent home to Germany by her father on his trips to Japan. '*Greetings from…!* symbolises the fragmentary memory I have of letters written by my Dad on his journeys to Japan. A colourful, exotic and still fascinating world for me! Each of the original Japanese stamps in these necklaces stands for its own travel tale, from Japan into my jewellery.'

'Nothing is lost, nothing is created; everything is transformed. I found lost photos and I found lost objects, I transformed them, I covered them. I watch a dialogue between the visible and the invisible, the past and the present', Margarida Matos says of her work. In her series of brooches *Kaluptein I*, the word

'kaluptein' means 'to cover' in Greek, and is also the origin of the word 'apocalyptical'. She has partially covered old jewellery with white plastic so that it looks as if it has been hidden under a blanket of snow which is just starting to melt, leaving some parts exposed, hinting at the jewel beneath.

Her series *Kaluptein II* involves binding found objects over and over with cotton thread to make necklaces and brooches with strange bulges, suggesting a snake's body after it has swallowed something particularly large. This time we are given no clues as to the nature of the original object trapped in its cocoon of white cotton. Matos describes it as 'a process of transformation but also of veiling'.

Finding and using objects which are not of much use to anyone else, turning them into something wearable, desirable and beautiful with fairly minimal interventions can surely be counted as a sustainable way of making jewellery.

Kaluptein I, brooches, Margarida Matos, 2007. Found objects, plastic. Photo: Dominic Sweeny

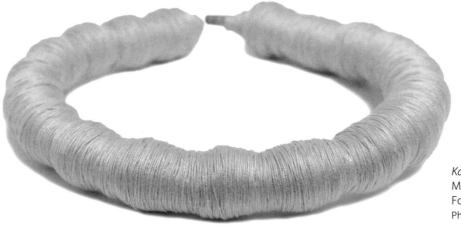

Kaluptein II, necklace, Margarida Matos, 2007. Found object, cotton. Photo: Dominic Sweeny

5 Conceptually Recycled

THIS CHAPTER looks at the possibilities for creating jewellery from the idea of a discarded object or material, rather than the object itself. It may be that, much as the maker would like to use something which they have found on the pavement or in the gutter, it would be impractical to use it for making jewellery for one reason or another. In this way, it becomes sustainable in thought, rather than in fact; it is the notion of the abandoned object which stimulates ideas for the piece of work.

Craig Isaac's *Royal Male* bracelets, inspired by the copious amounts of red rubber bands dropped by postmen each day, are a good illustration of this practice. The rubber bands are used to bundle up letters and, as these are delivered, the bands are cast to the ground, leaving a fresh trail marking the daily delivery of mail. When it came to making jewellery, Isaac found that the rubber perished on contact with ultraviolet light, so he set about finding a similar but more durable material, and came up with a mixture of natural and synthetic rubber. This material is made in a variety of strong colours and wears much better than natural rubber. The *Royal Male* title is a punchy play on words that is subtly laser-cut into the armbands.

Royal Male, bracelet, Craig Isaac, 2006. Laser-etched rubber band.
Photo: Craig Isaac

Ladbrokes

please ask our staff if you need help

broke

£

total stake £   :   p

all bets are subject to Ladbrokes rules

Broke Lad, pendant, Craig
Isaac, 2007. Plastic pen with
edited text, gold-plated nib
and chain.
Photo: Craig Isaac

In his *Broke Lad* pendants of 2006, Isaac follows a similar line of thought. Having noticed all the discarded, miniature ballpoint pens littering the floor of Ladbrokes betting-shops at the end of each day, he started to collect them. In an almost surgical operation, the pen nib is removed and the ink blown out, as you would blow an egg to keep the shell. The empty pen is drilled out at one end to receive a length of chain. The clever addition of a small round link allows the chain to be adjusted at any point and locked into place by gravity. The pound sign poised at the tip of the pen was rapid-prototyped and then cast in silver, making something precious from a cheap, disposable item. Isaac maintains that 'it's about ownership'; as with the rubber bands, he takes something which is free, hijacks the brand by changing it, and thereby makes it his own. Once again, the play on words in the title adds a sense of irony to the piece.

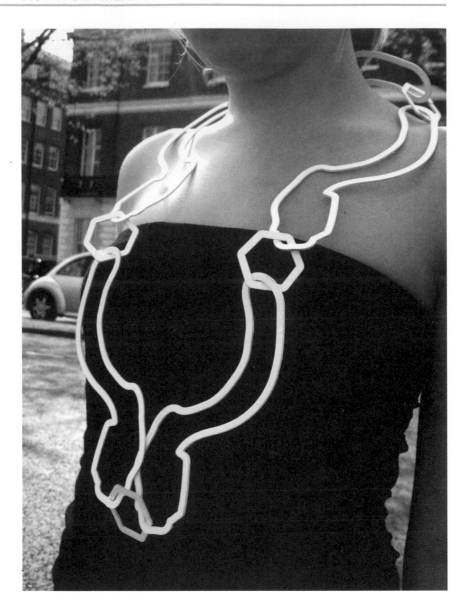

Lost Souls of London,
necklace, Claudie Fenwick,
Laura James, Lucy Roberts,
Saufun Kan, 2007.
Laser-cut card.
Photo: Laura James

Lost Souls of London was a collaborative work by a group of four Middlesex jewellery students. Walking around Central London's busy streets, the students looked out for odd, small objects they found lying on the ground. They outlined the objects with chalk, as if they were dead bodies at the scene of a crime, and took photographs of them in black and white. This lent a cinematic ambience to the proceedings, like a scene from a 1930s detective film. The shapes of the outlines were then laser-cut from card to make bracelets and neckpieces. Finally, the group returned to the scene of the crime to photograph the finished work on the exact spot where the original objects had been found.

The numerous butterfly-earring fittings that Lin Cheung found in her mother's jewellery box after she had died, gave her the idea of making earrings and necklaces from something which is normally just a fixing device, turning them into jewellery which is both poignant and funny. A parallel could be drawn here with some of the paintings of Antoni Tàpies, which explore the idea that the back of a painting can be as worthy of the viewer's interest as the front.

Although Cheung found a surprising number of butterfly fittings in the jewellery box, they were all odd ones. Thus there were only enough to make the first pair of *memoria* ear-pins, and more had to be bought to make the editions of necklaces and earrings which followed on from the original idea.

A jewel box belonging to her mother was also the starting point for a series of jewellery by Kate Maconie. She made a cuttlefish casting of one of her late mother's rings which had particular emotional significance for her. It was cast using a process whereby the ring is pressed into the impressionable inside material of the cuttlefish, which has

memoria, Editions, ear pieces, Lin Cheung, 1999. 18 ct gold, silver. Photo: Lin Cheung

BELOW *Seven out of Fifteen Rings,* Kate Maconie, 2007. Cast silver. Photo: Kate Maconie

been split in half. Once the impression has been made, the ring is taken out and molten metal is poured into the remaining cavity, so the original ring is not destroyed. A cuttlefish casting would usually only be used once, as subsequent castings would not be sufficiently detailed. Maconie has worked with this knowledge to positive effect, casting the ring over and over again

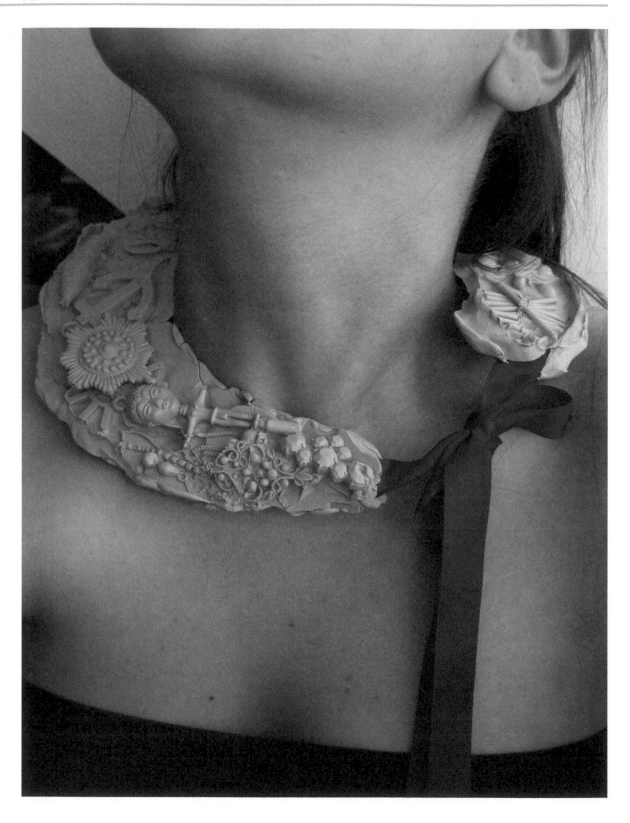

Yellow Gold, brooch,
Denise Julia Reytan, 2007.
Cast silicone.
Photo: Denise Julia Reytan

in the same mould until it becomes like a metal manifestation of the cuttlefish as the impression deteriorates. The resulting set of 15 rings provides both an intriguing insight into the process of an ancient method of casting and an emotional manifestation of the process of grief.

Denise Julia Reytan has used a different method of casting to make her jewellery. In contrast to Maconie's rings, which were cast in the round, these brooches and necklaces have a moulded front and a flat back, so that they sit well on the body but are almost like only half a piece of jewellery. All the decorative parts can be seen at the front of the piece, but the back is a blank surface. To get this effect, Reytan has used an open mould and poured silicone, rather than metal, into it. Her bold yellow brooch features an elegant antique necklace or brooch. It is quite a complicated piece, with pearls and other gemstones surrounded by fine, hanging, looped chains. Cast in silicone, the jewel is captured in minute detail and frozen forever into its background of spreading lemon-yellow silicone.

Casting or dipping would seem to be appropriate techniques for making conceptually recycled jewellery. In some forms of casting, the original object, such as a leaf or a wax form, is burnt out of the mould to form a cavity for liquid material to be poured into. Another way to capture an

FACING PAGE *Melting Pot,* necklace, Denise Julia Reytan, 2007. Cast silicone, textile.
Photo: Denise Julia Reytan

T-Shirt Necklace,
Tina Echterhölter, 2005.
Cotton jersey, ribbed jersey,
flock coating.
Photo: Tina Echterhölter

object in a different material is to dip a piece of lace or knitting into ceramic slip, so that when it is fired in a kiln at high temperature the fabric burns away, leaving a piece of ceramic lace in its place. Something flexible is replaced with a rigid version of itself.

Inspired by the idea of the juxtaposition of an old sweatshirt being worn with a traditional antique necklace, Tina Echterhölter has remade an area surrounding the distinctive neck of a sweatshirt so that it looks as though it has been cut out of an old one. She has printed silhouettes of traditional antique necklaces onto them to create an effect reminiscent of those 1960s knitted polo necks, known as dickies, which were just the truncated neck part of a sweater to be worn under a shirt or pullover.

Artist Julie Westbury's earlier work used old postcards, while a subsequent series of wall-based *Madonnas* were made from spirals of the same postcard, repeated and arranged so that a particular area formed a pattern. By making her own postcards of seaside views in the tradition of the mass-produced postcards one might expect to see on sale in a holiday resort, she has total control over both the content of the image and the part of it she wants to reveal.

Westbury's series of *Pearl Necklaces* exemplify the term 'conceptual recycling': not only has the postcard been remade, but an image has also been reused and reinterpreted to make something else. The concrete 'cannon balls' on the postcard are cleverly positioned in a spiral to look like a string of pearls, and the letterbox turns into a red ribbon. The whole construction is fastened together with a strong paper tape. In Westbury's own words, 'In these works, the photographic image becomes subordinate to the object. Images are obliterated and made abstract by repetition and manipulation'.

Although it might not be possible or desirable to use the original found object, it can still be the trigger for a whole host of creative thoughts and ideas. Something of sentimental value can be re-created without having to harm or destroy it. Equally, something which is seen by some to be of little value or importance can be the very thing which gets another person going.

Ramsgate Sands, postcard,
Julie Westbury, 2004.
A6 postcard.
Photo: Julie Westbury

*Child's Pearl and Red Ribbon
Necklace*, Julie Westbury,
2007. Ramsgate Sands
postcards.
Photo: Maria Militsi/Julie
Westbury

6 Useful Objects
and things which might come in handy

THIS CHAPTER considers how everyday domestic objects, found around the house or at a local hardware shop, can be used to make jewellery. We are surrounded by a plethora of fabulous gadgets and other contraptions, most of which have a built-in obsolescence. Often they are made of plastics of one sort or another, many of which are non-biodegradable, or may take a very long time to biodegrade. When mass-produced objects such as these break or their contents have been used up, they are sometimes kept because it seems a pity to throw them away, or because they cannot be easily recycled using household recycling facilities, or because they just might come in handy. *Home-Made* is a book about how Russians have used their ingenuity to adapt and modify old objects to make useful items, such as a bath plug made from a bent fork and a rubber-boot heel, or a doormat made out of metal beer-bottle tops; the book's author, Vladimir Arkhipov, has a collection

Soy Fish Brooches, Anon., 2008. Plastic soy-sauce bottles.
Photo: Jack Cole

Rubber Bracelets, Beppe
Kessler, 1981–2008.
Synthetic rubber, wire.
Photo: Beppe Kessler

of over a thousand such items. Other things, though humble, like old toothbrushes or empty sweet dispensers are appealing because they are manufactured in the most vivid colours, or because they have a clever opening mechanism. The clothes peg, which comes in so many shapes and forms is a good case in point: aside from its intended purpose of hanging up washing, it has far too many uses to be thrown away.

Yvonne Joris's book *Jewels of Mind and Mentality* discusses the renowned Dutch jeweller Marion Herbst's fascination with transforming everyday objects like shower hoses and salad baskets into bracelets or necklaces. Herbst's chrome *Shower Hose* bracelets from 1969 are used to illustrate this in the book. After Herbst died her husband Berend Peter Hogenesch gave a collection of her materials and some unfinished ingredients for pieces to another jeweller, Karin Seufert, to make new work from. This was a fitting tribute to Herbst, and a constructive way of ensuring that new jewellery would come from the raw materials she had collected. Another example from the book is Lous Martin's *Do it Yourself Kit,* 1974 for a necklace or bracelet made out of aluminium and pipe cleaners.

Also in the 1970s, Maria Hees and Marga Staartjes were making innovative brooches and bracelets out of plastic hairbrushes and scouring pads. Maria Hees's brushes attached to clothing in an unusual, but very practical way. The plastic brush spikes pushed through from the inside of a knitted jumper produced an effect of pinpoints of colour on the outside. They appeared sprinkled, yet contained, in a geometric shape within the surface of a knitted or loosely woven garment. In 1981, Beppe Kessler constructed substantial, sturdy, three-dimensional, twisted bracelets out of rubber bands, which were later replaced with industrial O-rings.

It is possible that these were born more out of the desire to take easily recognisable, utilitarian objects and use them in a different way, than with recycling in mind. Nevertheless, they are interesting in a sustainable context and they help to put the use of this kind of artefact into a historical perspective. They have obviously proved popular, as Kessler continues to make and market these bracelets today. They also set a precedent for younger designers like Sarah Crawford, who has used materials such as toothbrush heads combined with hand-dyed translucent nylon sheet to

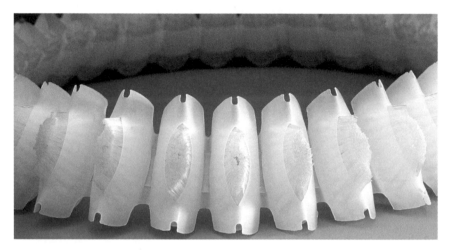

Toothbrush Necklace,
Sarah Crawford, 1994.
Toothbrush heads,
nylon sheet.
Photo: Richard Stroud

Toothbrush Bracelet,
Sarah Crawford, 1994.
Toothbrush heads,
nylon sheet.
Photo: Richard Stroud

make necklaces, earrings and brooches. In these pieces, the nylon provides a complementary smooth surface to the areas of bristles. Toothbrush handles have also been filed and transformed to make decorative joining systems for brooches. More recently, Crawford has used a variety of other useful objects to make bags and screens as well as jewellery. She too is attracted by the sort of everyday materials and objects one might find in a hardware shop, such as cable ties and O-rings, as these are useful for their joining possibilities. As Crawford explains, 'The visual qualities of a join are as important as the constructional ones. Joins are part of the surface of a piece, never hidden, and often the only decoration'. All her work is made using hand tools, which she maintains allow her a freedom that machinery does not.

Attracted by their colours and textures, Anemone Tontsch has made kitchen-pan scrubbers into brooches that look as if they might be edible. They are like miniature, striped towers of pink and turquoise Liquorice Allsorts sweets.

Tontsch has also made jewellery from many other readily available household objects, such as jam-jar tops, matches and tealight candles. There is a sense of immediacy and fun about her work, as though she takes a delight in finding uses for the mundane things which most people would throw away without hesitation once they are finished with.

Three Brooches,
Anemone Tontsch, 1991.
Pan scrubbers, silver.
Photo: Anemone Tontsch

Pendant, Anemone Tontsch, 2001. Soya bottle, knitted silver.
Photo: Anemone Tontsch

Necklace, Anemone Tontsch, 2007. Aluminium tealight holders, gold wire.
Photo: Anemone Tontsch

Coral Chain, necklace, Katja Korsawe, 1997. Rubber bands.
Photo: Thomas Schultze

Katja Korsawe's *Coral Chain* is made out of rubber bands which have been twisted and put together in such a way that the necklace does look remarkably like coral. In the following passage she gives a vivid glimpse into her thought process: 'In my bathroom I noticed a twisted-up hair band with some of my hair still in it, a used shape, in comparison to the originally untouched round form. This extreme change of shape interested me.' In the current version, she uses tightly twisted-up nylon tights, resulting in a necklace which looks as though it is made from curly astrakhan fur. According to Korsawe, there is no need for stitching together or fastening, as 'The spandex content lets the shape evolve. The necklace keeps sufficient elasticity to be able to pull it over the head'. The jaunty addition of the laundry label gives a clue as to her original starting point and material.

A group of bangles made by Eilean Somnitz are simple, precise and come in several lovely colours. They are made from the rubber seals used to make preserving jars airtight, and the addition of a coloured stone gives them that extra something that turns them from ready-mades into bracelets. It also begs the question about whether adding a stone makes an object seem more of a piece of jewellery in the wearer's eyes. Likewise, Somnitz has turned a set of rather dowdy towel fasteners into rings. They have been animated by placing a stone in their plastic jaws, so that, instead of having a mouthful of towel, they are used to grip a coloured stone.

I seem to have collected a vast amount of plastic bottle tops, partly because they come in a myriad of gorgeous colours and partly as potential material to make things from. For instance, certain soy-sauce bottle tops are made from a very strong plastic, which feels almost like Bakelite and is a rich orangey-red.

Strumpfhose Necklace, Katja Korsawe, 2008. Nylon tights. Photo: Thomas Schultze

Preserved Stones, bangles, Eilean Somnitz, 2003. Rubber jar seals, stainless steel, stones. Photo: Daniel Taubert

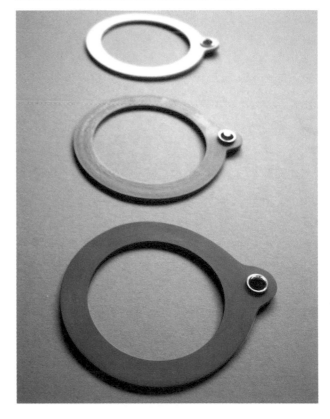

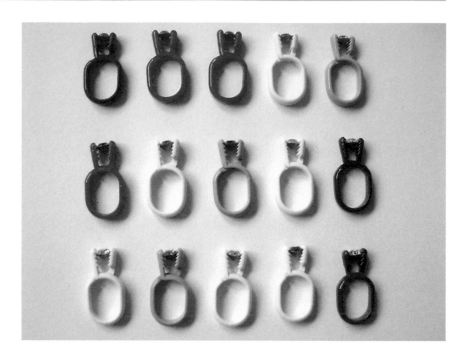

Rings, Eilean Somnitz, 2003. Plastic towel fasteners, coloured stones.
Photo: Daniel Taubert

The fact that they have two spouts makes them ideal for disguising the join of a piece of elasticated cord to make a necklace or bracelet.

Similarly, Ecover, the ecologically friendly range of household cleaning products, has bottle tops in a good translucent colour range. Some fit into each other or have hinged lids, offering a possible means of attaching them to clothing or of linking them together.

Smile Plastics have found a constructive way of recycling shampoo containers, yoghurt pots and mobile phone covers. The company manufactures panels from a variety of discarded household plastics, using a heat process which causes the colours to distort and blur into swirls of impressionist colour. This material has been used to make furniture, light fittings and signage, it could be used equally effectively in making jewellery.

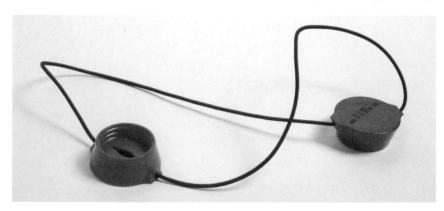

Soy Necklace, Julia Manheim, 2006. Soy-sauce tops, elastic cord.
Photo: Anthony Coleman

Lepidoptera Domestica is a collection of 683 domestic objects from 10 different countries put together by Manon van Kouswijk. It includes dustpans, soapboxes, cutlery, mugs and funnels, mostly made out of coloured plastic. Out of each piece she has cut the shape of a certain species of butterfly. These shapes have all been assembled and photographed, much as a Victorian lepidopterist might have ordered and arranged the specimens of their butterfly collection. An important part of this work is an artist's book that acts as a fanciful catalogue of the entire collection. It comes complete with a foldout wall chart of all the butterflies cut out from the objects and photographed in groups.

This is slightly reminiscent of early works by the artist Tony Cragg, in which he arranged and ordered a selection of found plastic objects and fragments into abstract areas of colour. This causes the viewer to do a double take, as it is almost impossible to discern whether the objects have been painted or have been grouped according to their original colour.

Lepidoptera Domestica, Manon van Kouswijk, 2005–07. Diverse materials. Photo: Uta Eisenreich

New Stones – Newton's Tones,
Tony Cragg, 1979. Found
plastic fragments. Arts
Council Collection, London.
Photo: Tony Cragg

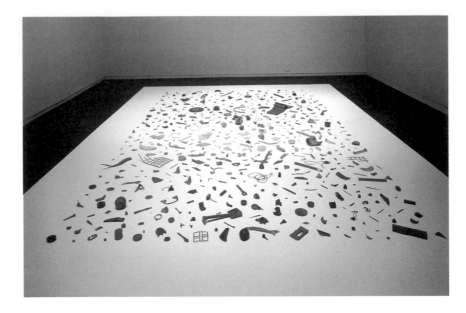

Safety Chain Necklace,
Nadia El-Sabei, 2006.
Safety pins, found buttons.
Photo: Aaron Tilley

Nadia El-Sabei's *Safety Chain* necklaces are made out of safety pins and buttons linked together to build up quite a complex 'nest'. They not only fasten to each other, but also help to keep found buttons safe, preventing them from getting lost again.

Recent jewellery by Esther Knobel also makes use of safety pins, which in this case have been extended with electroformed lumps and bumps grafted onto the simple, universally recognisable wire safety-pin. This treatment has turned them into insect-like forms resembling beetles or ladybirds, with bright enamelled colours, lending them a playful quality that brings to mind Dinky Toys.

Sigurd Bronger has made brooches, rings and necklaces by subverting tools or materials that are normally used as the means of making jewellery or other objects. For example, diamond fabric is usually used for polishing or sanding down extremely hard metal alloy implants for the medical industry. Bronger found that it was possible to buy the fabric, which is made from pieces of real diamonds, and have it cut accurately to any size. The silver brooch frame which he made to fit it was chrome-plated to reflect the diamond fabric and also to contrast with it. As Bronger explains, 'For me it was a way to incorporate many expensive stones into a piece of jewellery. In the sunlight the brooch gives out its full sparkle and 1,000 diamonds shine.'

Continuing along a similar trajectory, he has also incorporated a diamond drill bit into a brooch and a diamond-cutting disc into a necklace.

Brooches, Esther Knobel, 2002. Electroformed copper, enamel, safety pin.
Photo: Uri Gershuni

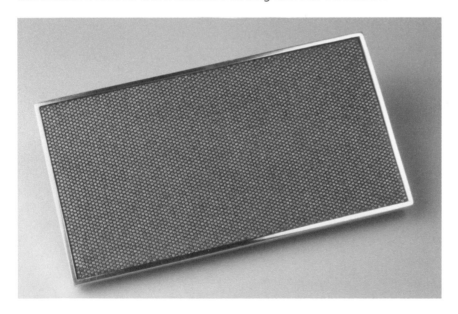

Big Diamond Brooch, Sigurd Bronger, 2006. Chrome-plated silver, real diamond-polishing linen, steel, 12 x 4 cm.
Photo: Sigurd Bronger

RIGHT *Diamond Necklace*, Sigurd Bronger, 2007. Real diamond-cutting plate, acrylic, silver, cotton cord, diameter 6 cm.
Photo: Sigurd Bronger

BELOW *Telephone Exchange Necklace*, 1994. Bakelite, leather. Collection: Leonora Robinson.
Photo: Anthony Coleman

Artist Leonora Robinson bought a necklace made of some of the Bakelite parts from an Australian telephone exchange that had been disbanded. The black, cog-like elements each have the numbers from 1 to 10 engraved around their outer edges, filled in with white in contrast to their shiny black background. She has re-strung them very simply on a black leather thong, making a sinuous necklace long enough to go over the head. Intriguing as a piece of jewellery, being made from unfamiliar objects that could be parts of a game or puzzle, the necklace also has a tactile, slinky quality.

A plain white cotton handkerchief is the starting point for Pierre Degen's series of photographic images. In itself, a white handkerchief can symbolise, or be used for, many different things. It could be knotted as a reminder, or worn as protection for the head from the sun. It might mean peace, or symbolise innocence and purity, as in a white wedding dress. Of course, it could always be used for blowing your nose. In Degen's powerful black and white images, a white cloth square has turned into a disturbing blindfold, with an imprint of a larger-than-life-sized eye placed on the exact spot where the eye would really be under the blindfold. Degen wrote about the

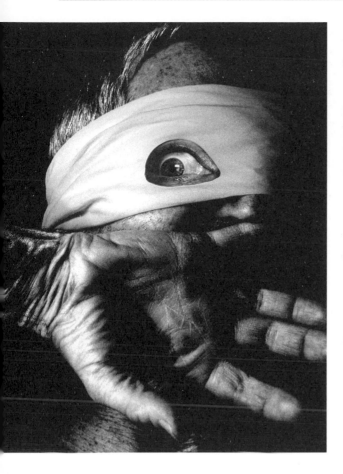 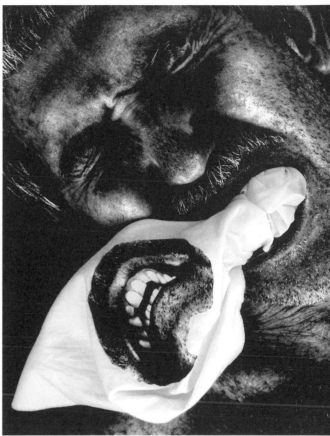

piece in the catalogue for the Maskerade exhibition, held at Galerie Ra, Amsterdam: 'The blindfold is the mask of the innocent children's game Blind Man's Buff and the mask of the condemned …'

In another image, the cloth has become a sort of gag, with the open mouth tumbling out of the real mouth. Degen's intention was to make images of a number of other uses for a hankie, such as a tourniquet or a cloth for polishing shoes.

Utilitarian things are easily obtained locally or found in the home. It is worthwhile saving them and keeping them to hand in case they do become useful. It just takes a bit of imagination and lateral thinking to find ways of converting them into jewellery, or of seeing other potential uses for them.

LEFT *Blindfold* …, Pierre Degen, Black and white photograph, 2004.
Photo: Pierre Degen

RIGHT *Gag* …, Pierre Degen, Black and white photograph, 2004.
Photo: Pierre Degen

7 Wearing It Out

THIS CHAPTER looks at jewellery which is transformed through being worn, or requires some form of change to enable it to be worn. This is a different type of reincarnation from that discussed in other parts of the book. In the normal course of events, everything tends to change through wear and tear, and different materials age in a variety of ways, even, like denim, becoming more desirable when they are faded and worn. Denim is referred to as being 'worn in' rather than worn out. Metals acquire a patina caused by changes and abrasions in surface or colour, wool starts to pill and textiles become thin or threadbare. Natural oils from the human body can help to preserve wooden jewellery through wearing it, whereas sometimes acids from the skin can instantly cause steel to rust and silver to tarnish.

On our city streets, layers of peeling posters pasted on top of one another are seen as a symbol of urban decay. But the distressed texture of their colour and pattern is also visually arresting. Corten steel, used outdoors for sculpture or in architecture, starts to rust almost immediately on contact with water. The steel continues to corrode until a certain point, whereupon it stops, remaining the same deep rusty red for many years. Similarly, if a floor is painted, walking on it gradually wears away the layer of paint to reveal the wood or concrete beneath. If wear and tear is considered a virtue worth keeping, it can be factored in to buildings, clothing and other artefacts as a lasting element, rather than something which needs to be replaced. Herein lies the claim for sustainability.

Some jewellery has been made with these types of changes in mind. Having been taken into consideration, they can then be used as a positive feature of the work. *Sediment Necklace* by Ruudt Peters is an example of this practice. Made of silver, it has been plunged into black paint, which clings to every surface of the necklace, gradually revealing more of the silver as it is worn.

Sediment Necklace, Ruudt Peters, 1995. Silver, black paint.
Photo: courtesy Chi ha Paura....?

It can be a challenge to make something which appeals at every stage of the transformation. Taking one form to start off with, another is revealed as the object comes into contact with movement or body heat, or as an outer layer is gradually worn away. This genre of jewellery begs to be worn, so that it can take on a different persona, just as the frog in a fairy tale longs to be kissed so that it can turn into a prince. The warmth of the body could turn a chocolate into a ring, or a diamond made of ice into a drop of water. A bar of soap gradually dissolving each time you wash might yield a hidden piece of jewellery, as in Manon van Kouswijk's string of pearls, which lies trapped in a bar of amber-coloured transparent soap, much as an insect can be seen caught in a real piece of amber. A connection could also be made here between having to use water to get to the necklace and having to dive through water to gather the pearls from which the necklace is made.

No Title – 'Soap', Manon van Kouswijk, 1995. Freshwater pearls, silk, glycerine soap.
Photo: Manon van Kouswijk

RIGHT *Rouwring*, a set of mourning rings, Miriam Verbeek, 1993. Silver, nut, silk, crochet.
Photo: Hennie van Beek

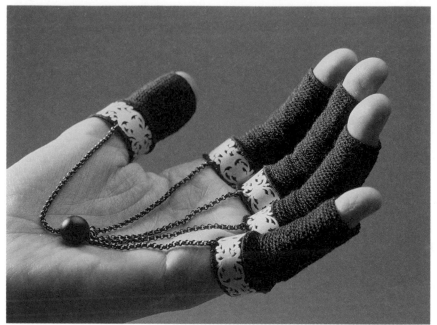

ABOVE *Wear-off Ring*, Miriam Verbeek, 1993. Silver, fine silk, crochet.
Photo: Hennie van Beek

This method of working is apparent in *Rouwring*, a set of mourning rings made by Miriam Verbeek in 1993. They are made from silver covered with fine black silk crochet, and are worn on the hand like a fingerless glove, with the tips of the fingers showing. The main part of the hand is also uncovered, with connecting threads from each finger culminating in a central nut which sits in the palm of the hand. As the rings are worn, the crochet starts to fray and unravel, revealing the silver rings beneath. This piece conveys a sense of journeying, from the darkness of the crochet through the process of grieving to the lightness of the exposed silver rings.

They are symbolic of the period of mourning after the death of a loved one, with the silver rings remaining as a permanent reminder of that person. In the Victorian period in Britain, mourning also went through different stages over about two years, each one bringing slight changes in the style of dress, colour and fabric a bereaved person was expected to wear. Verbeek has made several pieces in this vein: in *Wear-off Ring* again the crocheted fabric holding the piece together falls away, leaving a lasting part which symbolises the memory of the dead person. *Tears Collar* is made from car glass melted to form tiny balls, some of which are contained in a fragile nylon membrane surrounding the main necklace. The frill of nylon is intended to disintegrate when the collar is worn so that the necklace will cry glass tears.

There are a number of techniques used in metalwork, ceramics and textiles which are relevant to this way of working – for example, Japanese mokumé gané, where different-coloured metals are soldered together and then filed down to reveal the pattern they form. In ceramics, there are also techniques where the surface is taken away in places to reveal areas of other layers which lie or have been built up beneath. Some fabrics have been designed to turn different colours according to body heat or moisture. This has been used in clothing, as a fashion detail and also, on a more practical level, in babies' disposable nappies. Devoré is a way of etching fabric where a pattern is painted onto velvet with a mordant, which literally devours the nap of the material, leaving the fine woven cloth of the background with raised velvet patterning.

During her career, Dinie Besems has used a variety of materials to make jewellery which transforms in one way or another. In 1992 she made a necklace from ice and videoed the way it melted as it was worn. Many of her pieces take silver chain as a basis to work from, as it is very versatile in its ability to take on different forms. In a piece called *Never Naked Again*, a fine silver chain has been used as a device for measuring or plotting the area of a house, with symbols to mark corners, windows and doors, so that it could be reconstructed elsewhere as a 1:1 floor plan of the house; alternatively, the same length of chain can also be worn as a necklace if

Tears Collar, Miriam Verbeek, 1993. Silver, glass, nylon.
Photo: Hennie van Beek

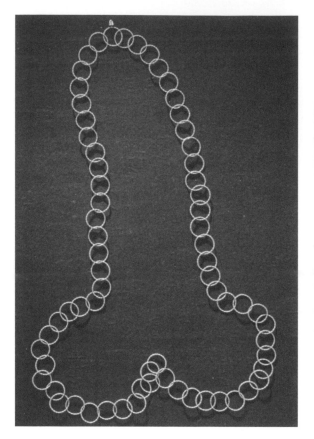

ABOVE *Kloteketting*,
Dinie Besems, 1993. Silver
chain, on a m² board (1 x 1 m)
Photo: Dinie Besems

ABOVE RIGHT *Chalkchain*,
Dinie Besems, 1994. Chalk.
Photo: Dinie Besems

wound around the neck a number of times. *Kloteketting* from 1993 is a simple chain composed of round silver links. Presented on a metre-square board, it outlines the shape of a phallus; when worn, however, it becomes an ordinary necklace with only a couple of tiny hints – an acorn and beaded wire – at its Jekyll and Hyde existence.

The *Chalkchain*, made a year later, is a long string of spherical beads carved from chalk, which leaves marks on the clothing as the wearer moves. Ultimately, the marks will turn into the jewellery as the chalk beads wear away, and then, presumably, the marks could be washed out of the clothing, so in the end the only remnant will be the thread which held the beads together from the beginning.

In *Exhaled Schoolhouse,* artist Cornelia Parker covered a school building in a series of chalk marks. The piece was made in 1990, when teachers still used chalk on blackboards (since superseded by electronic whiteboards). The beauty of the installation lay in its visual presence and its reference to the thousands of chalk marks made over the years in the building, while there was also the added poignancy that the rain and weather would gradually erase the marks over time.

Crown Jewels: Diamond Necklace, Suzi Tibbetts, 2006. Glass bottles, silver.
Photo: Suzi Tibbetts

Suzi Tibbetts describes her *Crown Jewels: Diamond Necklace* as 'a contemporary piece of interactive art made from recycled cider bottles. The silver chain is preserved inside the bottle until you choose to wear the necklace. By removing the crown top with a bottle opener, it is transformed into a pendant'.

She has also made a series of cast, black, wax lockets, which encase and protect a fragment of silver. Through being worn, they become imbued with meaning, but with calculated irony: they are at the same time being gradually worn away to expose the small silver fragment hidden within.

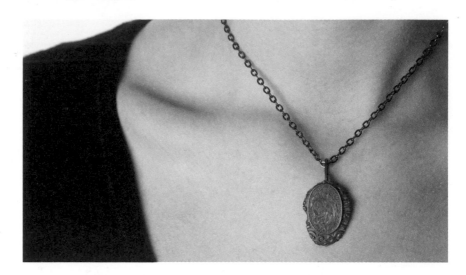

Forget Me Not, locket
pendant, Suzi Tibbetts, 2007.
Silver, wax, iron.
Photo: Suzi Tibbetts

The physical properties of ice make it an appropriate choice of material for this section of the book. But it is also very problematic to work with, particularly for making jewellery, as it starts to melt the instant it is taken out of the freezer, makes contact with the body, or is exposed to photographic lights. There is also the danger of ice burning the skin if it remains in contact for too long, although marks made on the skin in this way could be considered an important part of the work. Despite the difficulties of using ice as a medium, Naomi Filmer has embraced the challenge it poses and used it very successfully in *Be-hind, Be-fore, Be-yond*, a series of beautifully choreographed ice works.

Camphor is an unusual material to work with if you can withstand its strong smell and numbing anaesthetic properties. Japanese jeweller Shinichiro Kobayashi, has used the white, crystalline resin, which comes from Asian and Australian laurels, to make a necklace which melts and re-shapes itself during wearing. It is beautiful-looking in its pristine state, with roughly hewn, chunky, slightly sparkling white discs. It could come in very handy to hang up in your wardrobe, as camphor is known to be an effective moth repellent and is used to make mothballs.

Just as the life cycle of a butterfly goes through several stages, Richard Wilson's sculpture *Butterfly* underwent a series of transformations. He bought a scrapped Cessna light aircraft, reassembled it and then crushed it into a ball. The crushed plane was suspended from the ceiling of the old Wapping Pumping Station (now the Wapping Project gallery). Over a period of four weeks, he and a group of helpers unfurled and pulled out the squashed aluminium with hand-operated tools and straps. When they had finished and it resembled a crumpled version of the original plane, it was unhooked from the ceiling and allowed to crash nose down onto the gallery floor.

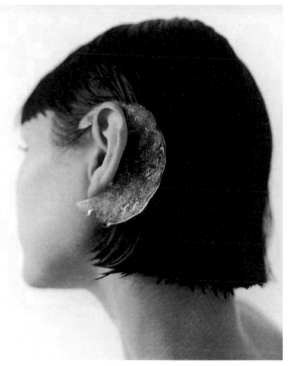

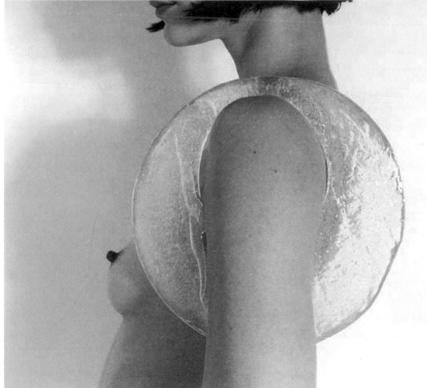

ABOVE LEFT *Ice-Upright Hand*,
Naomi Filmer, 1999. Ice.
Photo: Nicola Schwartz

ABOVE *Ice Ear-Behind*, Naomi
Filmer, 1999. Ice.
Photo: Nicola Schwartz

LEFT *Ice Under-Arm*, Naomi
Filmer, 1999. Ice.
Photo: Nicola Schwartz

Butterfly, Richard Wilson,
Wapping Project Space,
London, 2003.
Cessna light aircraft.
Photo: Richard Wilson

The process had been carefully documented throughout, and the edited time-lapse film was projected onto a screen which partially hid the crashed plane.

Textile designer Rebecca Earley is concerned with how printing and the production of textiles impacts on the environment. She only prints as much fabric as she intends to make up, and has produced clothing which is actively intended to improve with wear. Some of her designs take into account areas where there might be sweat marks – in order to accommodate them, make them a more acceptable part of the clothing, or to give the clothing a longer life.

The combination of chains and firecrackers conjures up a tough image, but Leonie Philpot has put them together in an extravagantly long, celebratory necklace which to look at is more 1920s Flapper than Heavy Metal. It is not mandatory to pull the crackers in order to wear the necklace, but it changes the complexion of the piece forever once the deed has been done. Perhaps the necklace should be kept intact until a suitably joyful moment, just as crackers are pulled on Christmas Day or at New Year, or maybe they will explode anyway as they rub against each other with wear, like two sticks rubbing together to make a spark.

There are sustainable plus-points for making jewellery which takes into account the possibilities thrown up by wear and tear, and uses them in a constructive way. However, making ice consumes energy, and freezers, along with fridges, are notoriously difficult to dispose of when they stop working. But then it also takes energy to get a raw material like chalk out of the ground. Apparently, although natural deposits of chalk have been quarried since prehistoric times and it is used as a basis for medicines, cosmetics, building materials and as an agricultural aid, it is now being replaced with a variety of chemicals. It is not clear whether this is because it is too expensive to continue to quarry the real thing, or because natural deposits are being used up. However, it does seem unwise to use chemicals as a substitute, as these will ultimately become pollutants.

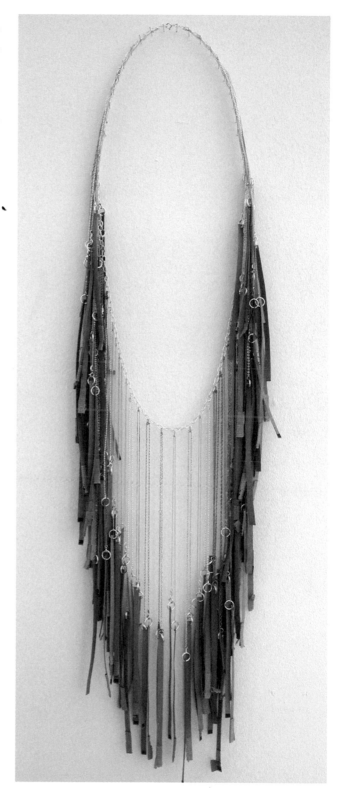

Cracker Banger Neckpiece, Leonie Philpot, 2006. Cracker pulls, silver.
Photo: Leonie Philpot

8 Found in Nature

THIS CHAPTER looks at jewellery made from natural materials, in terms of the previous lives of those materials as parts of living organisms, whether animal, vegetable or mineral. Everything in nature is there for a particular purpose and we interfere with its systems and patterns at our peril. Most of the examples of jewellery in this chapter fall into three main categories. The first includes those found in a domestic environment, such as bones, fruit stones and animal or human hair. The second group, including stones, leaves or feathers, is found in the natural debris of a wider landscape. The third category includes materials such as seeds and shellfish which have been farmed and harvested in an environmentally friendly way. The Pitt Rivers Museum in Oxford has a beautifully constructed Inuit waterproof parka in its collections, made of translucent seals' intestines sewn together. Nothing would have been wasted after hunting and killing a seal; every part would have been used to provide food, warmth, clothing, light and possibly jewellery.

Heavy Necklace,
Peter Hoogeboom, 1993.
Cobblestones, iron, glass.
Photo: Henni van Beek

Mourning Necklace for a Season (Winter), Peter Hoogeboom, 1993. Slate, silver, string. Box; autumn leaves. Photo: Henni van Beek

Natural materials inspired the first body adornment, and the examples are too numerous to mention. Anyone can make a daisy chain, or string some seashells together, but the focus here is on jewellery with a strong sense of design and concept.

In the 1970s David Poston made a necklace for an elephant from large rocks, perhaps an ironic take on diamonds being a girl's best friend, and a genuinely exciting new idea at the time. Peter Hoogeboom's *Heavy Necklace* from 1993 is made from cobblestones found on the beach at Ierapetra on the Greek island of Crete. Combined with iron and glass, it could well be a distant relative of Poston's elephant necklace. The fact that the exact place where the stones were found is detailed indicates the importance he attaches both to the find and its context. The necklace is also 'heavy' with religious symbolism.

A love of travel and ethnographical objects from faraway places are major influences on Hoogeboom's work. 'In my jewellery I try to put as much eloquence as is to be found in an Inuit carved horn spoon or a worn rattan Indonesian lunch basket'. This is evident in his ability to make jewellery which resonates with a strong spiritual presence. Hoogeboom has used many different natural materials in his jewellery, including shells,

Silk Trade, necklace, Peter
Hoogeboom, 1993. Silver,
slate from the roof of the
Rijksmuseum, thread, silk.
Photo: Henni van Beek

bone and poppy seeds. These are usually combined with metal and, more recently, porcelain. In a series of four pieces made in mourning for the seasons, The *Winter* necklace hibernates, snugly spiralled in a box made of autumn leaves. The leaves have been pressed together to form a box which is like a primitive forerunner of the moulded packaging now used to keep fruit from becoming damaged.

Other works make use of pieces of slate blown off the roof of the Rijksmuseum during a violent storm. Born and bred in Holland, Hoogeboom sees this as being particularly relevant to his work, as the museum exhibits the heritage of the Dutch as seafaring traders. He has often used the boat shape as a metaphor for travel and the voyage of life.

Cork has been the subject of a recent Portuguese jewellery symposium, which convened under the title *2nd SKIN*. Cork oak trees are grown in Portugal on a major scale, and the material which comes from them is vital to the Portuguese economy. Cork forests also provide a habitat for wildlife and a renewable resource of biodegradable, environmentally friendly material. Now that corks for wine bottles are often made from plastic, or have been replaced with screw tops, there is a decline in the cork market, and new ways are being found to sustain it. Furniture, shoes and even cricket balls are being manufactured from it, and the fashion for natural cork flooring is coming back again. Perhaps when the realisation gets through that plastic corks do not biodegrade easily – although admittedly there is some debate about this – manufacture of natural ones may resume.

There are a number of initiatives to find vegetable substitutes for leather with which to make shoes and bags – for instance, by recycling the rubber from tyres, and also using bamboo, hemp or cork. In 1985, Paul Derrez made a necklace of large, carved egg-shaped cork 'pebbles', bound together with red thread. At the time it was an unusual choice of material for jewellery, while still remaining wearable. As he describes it, 'The necklace is made from cork blocks, which are already made from layers of cork, glued together. They are used by painters for folding sandpaper around, to have a better grip. In those days it already became hard to find them. Now those blocks are pressed out of cork bits'. Derrez has also carved sizeable trays, bowls and other objects out of the same material. These have strictly defined, geometric forms, whereas the *Pebble Necklace* has softer, more organic shapes.

Cork has been used in a completely different way by Verena Sieber-Fuchs, to make a collar which looks as though she has thrown a fine net around a myriad of tiny cork pieces to prevent them from floating away. The practical references to fishing nets studded with corks are overtaken by

Pebble Necklace, Paul Derrez, 1985. Cork, textile.
Photo: Tom Haartsen

Keep the Soul Warm, collar,
Verena Sieber-Fuchs, 1987.
Wine corks, inox knitted.
Photo: Sebastian Sieber

more glamorous overtones in this piece, its almost invisible construction
giving it a sensuous fluidity.

Mango or avocado stones are such beautiful shapes that I find it difficult
to throw them away. Who has not delighted in watching a bean or a pip
sprout and grow? It is a magical thing. The best way of disposing of
vegetable and fruit waste is to compost it. This is another form of magic, as
the green stuff that goes into a compost bin is transformed over time into
rich dark earth. In nature, the way in which animals and birds eat fruit and
discard the seeds, pips and stones is a way of propagating the seed to grow
next season's fruit. Since prehistoric times, humans have not only enjoyed
eating fruit, but have also used the seeds to decorate themselves, as a
means of bartering and as an early form of money.

Contemporary versions include Hans Stofer's *All Souls Ring,* with olive
stones and a blackened steel-wire and glass construction which forms a
cage around the stones. This could indicate a desire to keep them safe
when they would normally be spat out and discarded, or to imprison them,
thereby taking away any potential for growth.

FACING PAGE *Agave Big Bos*,
necklace, Bas Bouman, 2005.
Sisal, bone, tea (for
colouring).
Photo: Bas Bouman

Bas Bouman has made necklaces with titles like *Relics of Future Memories* using cherry stones combined with calf bone and sisal. The materials for this and the other pieces in a collection called *Treasures from a Todays Huntingspot* came from food purchased at a local supermarket, his own personal hunting ground. It was important to him that the jewellery was made from the bones and fruit stones left over from food he had cooked and eaten himself. This is a comment on what Bouman perceives as the uncaring way in which food is bought, prepared and eaten, with little knowledge of where it has come from, or how it has been produced. The references to hunting in his work also tie in to ethnic jewellery and the significance and value attached to various materials – in Bouman's words, 'a tooth from the first bear you shot, a claw from a tiger to show your braveness, a piece of skin to protect you'. Certainly, his work has a primitive, tribal quality to it, and he uses it as a vehicle to make a serious point with some irony and humour.

ABOVE *All Souls Ring*, Hans Stofer, 1994. Blackened mild steel, glass, olive stones. Crafts Council Collection, London. Photo: Sara Morris

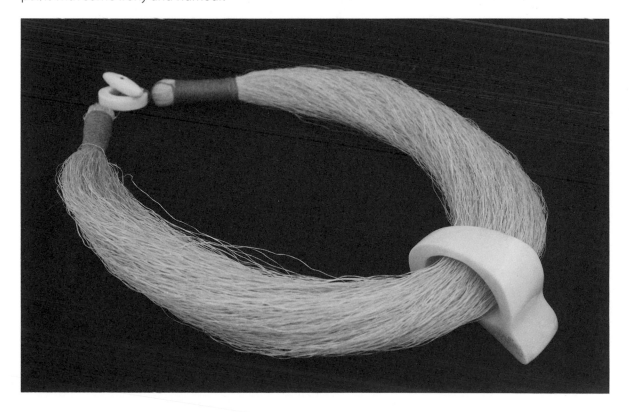

Brazilian potter Maria Donato and business partner Ana Smaldon have formed a company making jewellery from exotic Brazilian seeds which are all ethically sourced. They are collaborating with Pacova, a womens' co-operative in Mato Grosso in the centre of Brazil, to produce necklaces, belts and bags, enabling the local women to transfer their existing, traditional skills to make jewellery using the familiar native seeds and pods that they have grown up with.

The seeds they use are tremendously varied in shape, form and colour. They all have different properties and meanings. Some, like the tucum coconut, are black and lustrous. This is the edible seed of the chambira palm, whose leaf fibres are used to make string for bags, hammocks and musical instruments. Tucum strings are regarded by the Indians as powerful, protective charms against forest spirits.

Others such as the *angelim do brejo*, or money-fruit pods, are like dried leaves in rich autumnal colours. The tree that bears them grows along riverbanks and provides nourishment for the fish during the monsoon period. The jatoba pod comes from a massive canopy tree which produces resin used in pottery glazes, wine and magic rituals. The pod is used to make a nutritious flour.

FACING PAGE, TOP *Big Bone*, necklace, Bas Bouman, 2005. Bone, bamboo.
Photo: Bas Bouman

FACING PAGE, BOTTOM *Caramel Zebra*, necklace, Bas Bouman, 2005. Apricot stones, calf bone, bamboo, coconut, sisal.
Photo: Bas Bouman

BELOW *Jatoba and Silver Bead Necklace*, M+A Designs, 2008. Jatoba seed, silver.
Photo: Anthony Coleman

BOTTOM *Tucum and Silver Studs Necklace*, (detail) M+A Designs, 2006. Tucum coconut, silver.
Photo: Anthony Coleman

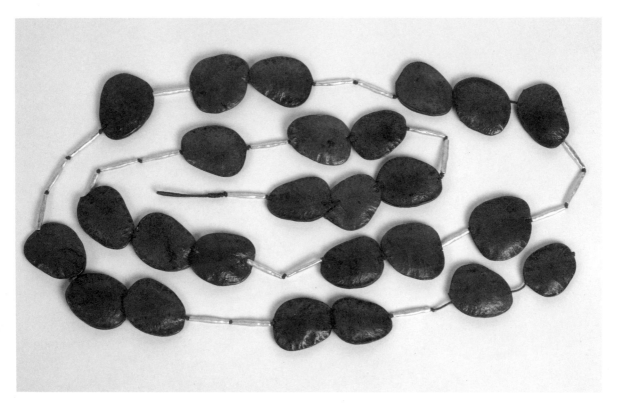

Angelim and Silver Necklace,
M+A Designs, 2007. Angelim
do brejo pod, silver
Photo: Anthony Coleman

All these seeds need to be oiled to keep them from drying out, as they will naturally start to crack in order to sprout and grow. Wearing them helps to prevent cracking as they absorb oil from the skin. They have been worked on in a variety of ways, inlaid with small silver studs and tiny circles of silver tube, or strung together with a contrasting cast silver bead. What distinguishes this jewellery from other strings of beads is the way that they have been put together and finished with an eye to design aesthetics.

Owner's Manual is a book about Warwick Freeman's jewellery and the people who own it. In it, Julie Ewington writes about a brooch of his called *Water Cross*. It is made from baler, a shell so huge that, as its name suggests, it was used for baling seawater out of boats. 'It once sheltered an enormous mollusc, but in another life has carried freshwater on land …' Like a talisman or amulet, Freeman's jewellery seems to connect with the ancient, while remaining within a contemporary format. His *Large Star* mother-of-pearl brooch from 1990 is a good example of this. The star form has become his personal emblem, since he has made so many different versions of it. It comes from the star shape that is made by putting both outstretched thumbs and forefingers together and looking at the space between them. The *Large Star* brooch makes particularly sensitive use of the ripples and whorls which occur like echoes of the sea in mother-of-pearl shell.

Large Star, Warwick Freeman,
1990. Pearl shell, lacquer,
w. 60mm.
Photo: Patrick Reynolds

Lattice Brooch, Warwick
Freeman, 1994. Cow bone,
w. 67mm.
Photo: Patrick Reynolds

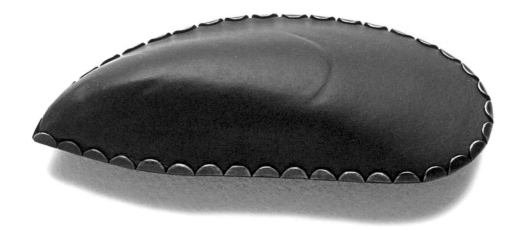

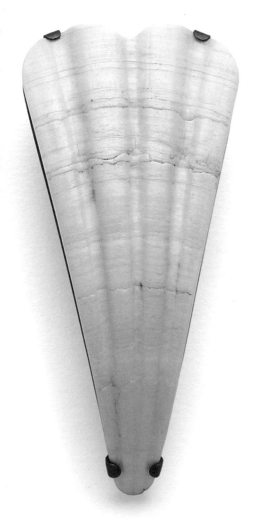

LEFT *White Heart*, Warwick Freeman, 2000. Scallop shell, silver, l. 80mm.
Photo: Patrick Reynolds

ABOVE *Muscle*, Warwick Freeman, 2000. Mussel, shell, lacquer, silver, l. 87mm.
Photo: Patrick Reynolds

Freeman uses many other types of shells and bones in his work. His current thinking is that 'The issues around sustainability and "natural" materials are as complicated as those around "unnatural" materials'. He is aware that although most of the shells he uses are being farmed commercially, making their supply sustainable, the way in which they are being farmed may not be so sustainable.

Tania Clarke-Hall has recently started using leather to make necklaces and bracelets. She is happy to work with it in the knowledge that it comes from animals which have been slaughtered for food and have not just been bred for their hide. The material she uses has been tanned with vegetable tanning, which is more environmentally friendly than a chemical-based alternative. She finds leather to be the perfect medium with which to express the unexpected, given that, as she puts it, 'leather is almost always portrayed with smart, polished surfaces and edges'. Instead, one edge of a long dark strip is cut into and painted with bright colour inside the cuts, the contrasting colour being only fully revealed when the necklace is put on. Another necklace looks like a neatly formed row of silhouetted black beads, but is laser-cut so that the fibrous edges of the leather are intentionally exposed.

Cut Leather Necklace, Tania Clarke-Hall, 2007. Leather, acrylic paint.
Photo: Anthony Coleman

Sculptors Andy Goldsworthy and Richard Long are both well-known for their art in the landscape. Whilst each produces very different work, they both use only materials which are found in the particular landscape they choose to be in. In many of Goldsworthy's works, leaves might be joined together with thorns or grasses, and no extraneous materials are used. His work seems to exemplify the idea that one should take nothing from the land and leave nothing behind.

Black Beads, Tania Clarke-Hall, 2008. Leather, leather dye, brass.
Photo: Tania Clarke-Hall

ABOVE *Arrested Flight*, ring, Elisabeth Holder,
2002. Iron, feather.
Photo: Elisabeth Holder

ABOVE RIGHT *Second-Hand*, ring, Elisabeth
Holder, 2002. Cat's whisker, silver.
Photo: Elisabeth Holder

RIGHT *Second-Hand*, necklace, Elisabeth
Holder, 2002. Cat hair, silk, reused clasp.
Photo: Elisabeth Holder

Long's works tend to be more often assemblages of rocks or branches placed in a specific formation, with the act of walking another important element. He has also transposed areas of land from one part of Britain to another, exchanging completely different sets of soil and weather circumstances and monitoring the results. It is interesting to reflect upon what grows naturally or wild in a ring of turf from Scotland when this is placed within the context of a piece of land in Southern England. As with Warwick Freeman's work, a connection is being made between ancient and modern, both in nature and the landscape.

Prisoners of war held by the Japanese in the 1940s pulled out their own hair to make jewellery both as keepsakes and for bartering. Different-coloured strands of hair can be seen in the bracelets and necklaces that they made. Hair has been used in jewellery and mask-making for thousands of years and has long been associated with mourning jewellery. There are also a number of contemporary jewellers who choose to work with it. For instance, Elisabeth Holder has used various materials to make jewellery, but observes that animal or human hair 'undergoes a strange transformation when no longer connected to the body: it becomes dead matter, is considered filth and can easily arouse disgust'. However, she views the whiskers and hair shed by her cats as a positive gift and so has created a series of pieces called *Second-Hand*, including a ring made from a coiled cat's whisker and silver. She has also rubbed cats' hairs together to make a soft furry necklace of felted beads. These have been treated like precious pearls, threaded and knotted onto silk. *Arrested Flight*, an iron and feather ring, is an elegant way of capturing and making wearable a feather found after a cat had caught and eaten a bird. These works use a minimum of energy, apart from that needed to generate the idea and make the piece, and the materials are mostly free and found close to home.

FAR LEFT *Protection*, second-hand silver locket (partially covered), Dionea Rocha Watt, 2005/6. Human hair.
Photo: Dominic Tschudin

LEFT *Protection*, second-hand silver locket (covered), Dionea Rocha Watt, 2005/6. Human hair.
Photo: Dominic Tschudin

Loss, brooch, Dionea Rocha
Watt, 2006. Lace, human hair,
silver, lead, freshwater pearl,
6.5 x 8 cm.
Photo: Dionea Rocha Watt

BELOW *Loop*, necklace (detail),
Dionea Rocha Watt, 2007.
Plaited human hair,
18 ct gold.
Photo: Dominic Tschudin

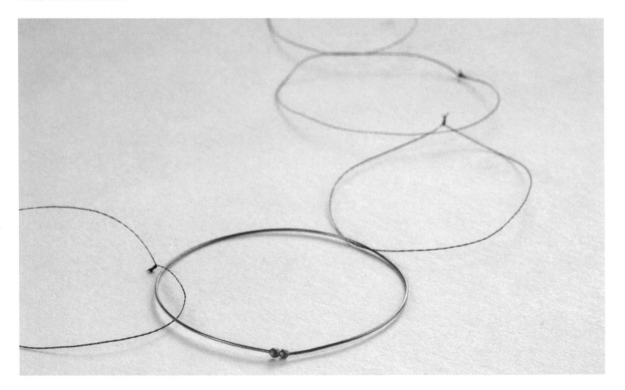

Dilston Grove, Ackroyd and Harvey, 2003. Grass, clay, water, light; sound by Graeme Miller. An installation in the Clare College Mission Church, Bermondsey, London (commissioned by LIFT in association with café Gallery Projects & Artsadmin). Photo: The artists

There is a visual connection between Dionea Rocha Watt's jewellery and the way that artists Heather Ackroyd and Dan Harvey make growing installations which cover buildings. Rocha Watt has covered a silver locket with her own hair, thus rendering the locket unwearable. This has resulted in an object which personifies something akin to wearing your heart on your sleeve: the usually secret contents of a locket are now clearly visible on the outside, practically obscuring the locket beneath. She too is aware of the strong reactions that hair can provoke when it is detached from the body, but notes that 'Hair is delicate and fragile but at the same time durable since it survives us and contains our DNA'.

Ackroyd and Harvey's vertical green walls defy gravity. They even managed to make grass grow in the dark interior of an old concrete church, Dilston Grove, in 2003, revitalising the disused, deconsecrated church and infusing it with new growth.

Anemone Tontsch has made grass grow on lace hats, but it would be an equally suitable site for growing any herb, hence its title *Invention for Cooks*. Spiky green tufts sprout out of the top of the wearer's head, just as a roof garden might sprout out of the top of a building.

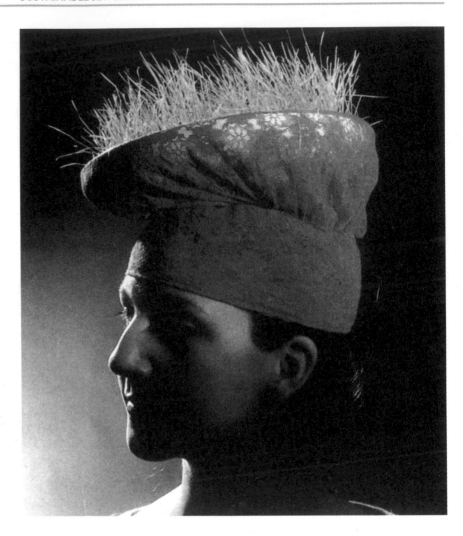

Invention for Cooks, hat,
Anemone Tontsch, 1986.
Frisbee, soil, grass.
Photo: Anemone Tontsch

FACING PAGE *Pigeon Wing
Adornment*, Rheanna
Lingham, 2005. Pigeon wing,
steel wire, ribbon.
Photo: Rheanna Lingham

Feathers found in specific places at specific times form the basis of Rheanna Lingham's necklaces. Her love of feathers began with plucking game birds and finding their feathers too beautiful to throw away. Her jewellery featured magnificent corsages and plumes of whole iridescent mallard wings, or necklaces of large spherical beads made from patterned pheasant feathers combined with chains, all of which lent an air of *fin-de-siècle* decadence and theatricality to the work. Recent work focuses on daily finds of feathers lying on the ground locally, on collecting them in envelopes marked with the date and place where they were found. Occasionally, the find would be massive, with, for example, the remains of a fight between a swan and a fox resulting in a huge white feather necklace. After three months the contents of each envelope were made into necklaces attached to a length of chain; a day without a find was marked by a plain gold chain.

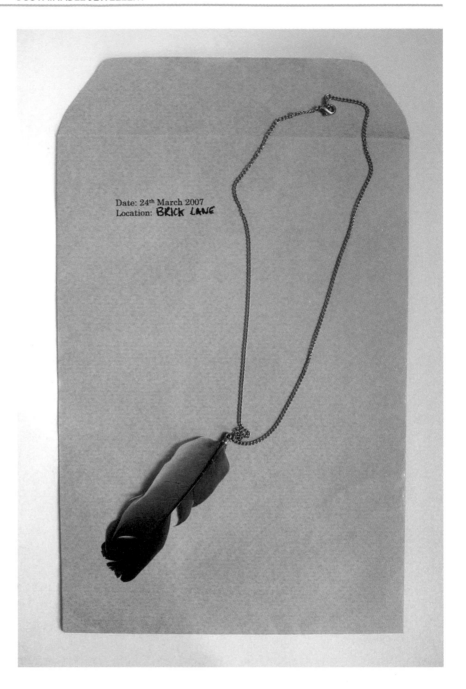

Date: 24th March 2007
Location: BRICK LANE

Found Feathers, necklace,
Rheanna Lingham, 2007.
Feathers, gold-plated chain.
Photo: Rheanna Lingham

Working with natural materials can put us in touch with the ancient and primitive. Nature can provide the means of creating something from the debris of a meal, or from the debris of a wider landscape which is in a constant state of growth and renewal. A slate blown off a roof in a violent storm or a cat's whisker found on the carpet can be equally stimulating in providing the impetus to make.

Conclusion

In conclusion, it goes without saying that sustainability is a subject fraught with contradictions. During the writing of this book, China has banned production of ultra-thin plastic bags in a campaign against 'white pollution'. This is good news and a step in the right direction, one would think, but as a consequence the largest plastic-bag manufacturer in China has had to close and 20,000 people have lost their jobs. The ban could also lead to a surge in the manufacture of higher-quality thicker plastic bags, which will use up more crude oil (currently estimated at five million tonnes each year) in their production and take even longer to biodegrade. There have been worrying reports that toxins leached from plastic waste are being found in fish in the Pacific Ocean, which in turn is affecting the food chain. This is just one example of the possible ramifications of a sincere attempt to address an environmental problem.

Being aware of how little is happening globally to promote sustainability, it would be easy to feel overwhelmed, panic-stricken and ineffectual. Bringing it down to a local level, it begins to feel slightly more manageable. Throughout the book there are examples of jewellery being made with materials sourced from closer to home: not diamonds from South Africa, but diamond paper from the local hardware shop. Also in its favour is jewellery's small carbon footprint: it is easily transportable and does not make a massive impact on the environment from that point of view. The negative side is that energy and chemicals are often used to make or document it, which is not so good, but as this is on a small scale, it is perhaps not too disastrous. What has become evident to me in the process of writing this book is the massive resource of imaginative thinking and making skills that exists amongst contemporary jewellery-makers, which can transform what would normally be regarded as worthless objects into beautiful things to contemplate, use or wear.

Single Ocado Blooms
FROM TOP *Cupboard Brooch*,
Freezer Brooch, *Fridge Brooch*,
Kristina Kitchener, 2008.
Each made from one Ocado
plastic bag.
Photo: Kristina Kitchener

Glossary

Angelim do brejo A Brazilian seed also known as the money-fruit pod.

Berlin iron Early 19th-century cast-iron jewellery resembling black lace.

Brundtland Commission United Nations, 1987. *Report of the World Commission on Environment and Development,* General Assembly Resolution 42/187, 11 December 1987.

Cabochon A rounded, unfaceted cut of a semi-precious or precious stone.

Casting The technique of pouring a liquid material into a mould so that it solidifies into the shape of the mould.

Cable tie A nylon strap used to fasten electrical cables to a surface. It cannot be untied but must be cut.

Ciro Pearls Ltd. A firm dealing in pearl jewellery established in 1917.

Corten steel A steel alloy developed to rust without reducing core strength.

Devoré A technique for patterning cloth by chemically removing one layer to expose another.

Dinky Toys Miniature model cars and trucks.

Dirty metals Metals which have not been ethically mined and produced and have not been sourced from reputable dealers.

Doming A technique of hammering a material (usually metal) with a rounded steel punch into a metal doming block to make the material into a semi-spherical shape.

Electroforming An electrical process for coating an object in a thin layer of metal.

Flocking An industrial coating technique of applying electrostatically charged fibres to an adhesive-coated surface, giving the effect of suede or velvet.

Jatoba pod A Brazilian seed used to make flour.

Laser-cutting A technological means of precision-cutting materials using laser and computer-aided design.

Lenticular A technology for making moving or 3-dimensional images.

Kimble A nylon tag used in shops to attach a price label to a garment.

Memento mori A reminder or warning of the certainty of death.

Mokumé gané A traditional Japanese technique of laminating metals to produce a 'wood grain' effect.

Ocado A supermarket delivery service.

O-ring A circle of rubber, round in section, manufactured as a seal or gasket for engines.

Pearly Kings & Queens Traditionally, costermongers (street sellers of fruit and vegetables) who wear clothing lavishly decorated with mother-of-pearl buttons.

Pyrography Technique of burning patterns into a material with a heated tip or wire.

Rapid prototyping The automatic construction of physical objects using solid free-form fabrication and computer-aided design.

Rub-over setting A plain metal setting made to fit a gemstone (or button).

Ruching Technique of gathering material to make folds or frills.

Silicone A type of rubber that can be cast and moulded, or used to make the mould itself.

Smile Plastics Panels made from recycled household plastics.

Spandex A stretchy synthetic fibre also known as elastene.

Sprüngli Swiss chocolate manufacturer.

Sustainability The characteristic of a process or state that can be maintained at a certain level indefinitely.

Tectan® Panels made from recycled drinks cartons.

Tucum coconut The edible seed of the chambira palm from Brazil.

Vanitas A reminder of the worthlessness of worldly goods.

Vegetable ivory Seed of the *Hyphaene Phytelephas* palm tree, it looks like ivory and can be worked in a similar way when completely dried out.

Bibliography

Archer, Michael, *Mona Hatoum* (London: Phaidon, 1997).

Arkhipov, Vladimir, *Home-Made: Contemporary Russian Folk Artifacts* (London: Fuel, 2006).

Barnes, Lucinda, *Tony Cragg: Sculpture 1975–1990* (London: Thames and Hudson in association with Newport Harbor Art Museum, 1991).

Brower, Cara, Mallory, Rachel & Ohlman, Zachary, *Experimental Eco-Design: Architecture, fashion, product* (Hove: Rotovision, 2005).

Change the World for a Fiver: We are What We Do (London: Short Books, 2004).

Callinicos, Elizabeth and Votalato, Gregory, *Heirlooms: An Exhibition of Rings*: Association for Contemporary Jewellery, 2006).

Cheung, Lin, Clarke, Becky & Clarke, Indigo, *New Directions in Jewellery II*, (London: Black Dog, 2006).

Cheung, Lin & Broadhead, Caroline, I in Cheung: *Jewellery and Objects* : Photo ED Press, 2005).

Dormer, Peter & Turner, Ralph, *The New Jewellery: Trends and Traditions* (London: Thames and Hudson, 1985).

Drutt English, Helen & Dormer, Peter, *Jewelry of Our Time: Art, Ornament and obsession* (London: Thames and Hudson, 1995).

Ferguson, Bruce & Morgan, Jessica, *Cornelia Parker*: Art Data, 2000).

Fraser, Simon, *Contemporary Japanese Jewellery* (London: Merrell Publishers in association with the Crafts Council, 2001).

Freeman, Warwick, *Owner's Manual: Jewellery* (Auckland: Starform, 1995).

Game, Amanda & Goring, Elizabeth, *Jewellery Moves: Ornament for the 21st century* (Edinburgh: National Museums of Scotland, 1998).

Goldsworthy, Andy, *Wood* (London: Viking, 1996).

Grant, Catherine, *New Directions in Jewellery* (London: Black Dog, 2005).

Joris, Yvonne G.J.M., *Jewels of Mind and Mentality: Dutch Jewelry Design 1950–2000* (Rotterdam: 010 Publishers, 2000).

Joris, Yvonne G.J.M., *Gijs Bakker and Jewelry* (Stuttgart: Arnoldsche, 2005).

Künzli, Otto, *Das dritte auge=The third eye=Let derde oog* (Amsterdam: Stedelijk Museum, 1991).

Le Van, Marthe, *500 Necklaces: Contemporary Interpretations of a Timeless Form* (New York: Lark, 2007).

Le Van, Marthe, *1000 Rings: Inspiring Adornments for the Hand* (New York: Lark, 2005).

Lim, Andy, *Karl Fritsch: Metrosideros Robusta* (Cologne: Darling Publications, 2006).

Milner, Alison, *Inspirational Objects: A Visual Dictionary of Simple, Elegant Forms* (London: A&C Black, 2005).

Nichte Ohne=pretty sharp: Scmuck, gerat, product=jewellery, implements, products: Arbeiten von Studierenden, Ehemaligen und Lehrenden aus dem Studiengang Produktdesign Fachhochschule Düsseldorf=works by past and present students and the current staff of the School of Product Design, Düsseldorf University of Applied Sciences (Stuttgart, Arnoldsche, 2002).

Phillips, Clare, *Jewels and Jewellery* (London: Victoria and Albert Museum, 2000).

Sandino, Linda, *Hans Stofer's Design Wilderness*, (Solothurn: Galerie SO, 2006).

Tàpies, Antoni, *Tàpies Communicacio Sobre el Mur* (Barcelona: Fundacio Antoni Tàpies, 1992).

Turner, Ralph, *Contemporary Jewellery: A Critical Assessment* (London: Studio Vista, 1976).

van Kouswijk, Manon, *Lepidoptera Domestica* (The Netherlands Foundation for Visual Arts, Design and Architecture, 2007).

Wilson, H., *Silverwork & Jewellery* (Bath: Pitman Press, 1971).

Contributing Artists and Useful Websites

ARTISTS

Ackroyd, Heather and Harvey, Dan — www.artsadmin.co.uk
Azumi and David — www.azumianddavid.com
Bagaki, Eleni
Bakker, Gijs — www.gijsbakker.com
Bartley, Roseanne — picasaweb.google.com.au/bartleybila/
RoseanneBartley

Baschta, Heike — www.fh-duesseldorf.de
Bell, Linsey
Besems, Dinie — www.diniebesems.nl
Boltanski, Christian — www.tate.org.uk
Borland, Christine — www.lissongallery.com
Bouman, Bas — www.klimt02.net
Broadhead, Caroline — www.bmgallery.co.uk
Bronger, Sigurd — www.sigurdbronger.no
Campana Brothers — www.campanas.com.br
Cheung, Lin — www.lincheung.co.uk
Clarke-Hall, Tania — item.rakuten.co.jp
Cook, Julie — www.julie-cook.com
Cornell, Joseph
Cragg, Tony — www.lissongallery.com
Crawford, Sarah
Cullivan, Millie
Darbourne, Rachel
de Quin, Rebecca — www.abds.co.uk
Degen, Pierre
Derrez, Paul — www.galerie-ra.nl
Earley, Rebecca — www.beckyearley.com
Eberle, Philipp
Echterhölter, Tina

Philpot, Leonie	www.leoniephilpot.com
Picasso, Pablo	www.fundacionpicasso.es
Planteydt, Annelies	www.galerie-ra.nl
Poston, David	www.lesleycrazegallery.co.uk
Potter, Laura	homepages.gold.ac.uk
Pritchard, Sarah	
Pröpstl, Barbara	
Ray, Man	www.manray-photo.com
Remy, Tejo	www.droogdesign.nl
Reytan, Denise Julia	www.fh-duesseldorf.de
Rezvani, Mahta	www.free-range.org.uk
Roberts, Lucy	
Robinson, Julian	
Robinson, Leonora	
Rocha Watt, Dionea	www.dionearochawatt.blogspot.com
Sajet, Philip	www.klimt02.net
Seufert, Karin	www.karinseufert.de
Sieber-Fuchs, Verena	www.galerie-ra.nl
Smit, Robert	www.louisesmit.nl
Somnitz, Eilean	www.eileansomnitz.de
Staartjes, Marga	
Stach, Gisbert	
Stofer, Hans	www.galerieso.com
Tàpies, Antoni	www.fundaciotapies.org
Tibbetts, Suzi	www.iclimbtrees.co.uk
Tontsch, Anemone	www.galerie-cebra.de
Urquhart, Donald	www.lochlomond-trossachs.org
van Kouswijk, Manon	www.galerie-ra.nl
Varney, Rachelle	
Verbeek, Miriam	www.galeriehelpuzelven.nl
Vilmouth, Jean-Luc	www.jlvilmouth.com
Walpole, Lois	www.loiswalpole.com
Wentworth, Richard	www.lissongallery.com
Westbury, Julie	www.artworkersguild.org
Williams, Nicola	
Wilson, Richard	
Zeldin O'Neill, Deborah	

WEBSITES FOR MATERIALS

Cork	www.acfnewsource.org
Durat	www.durat.com
Smile Plastics	www.smile-plastics.co.uk
Tectan	www.tectan.de
Wot-ever Scrapstore	www.wot-ever.org.uk

GALLERIES AND MUSEUMS

Association for Contemporary Jewellery	www.acj.org.uk
Crafts Council Collection	www.craftscouncil.org.uk
Fingers Gallery	www.fingers.co.nz
Foundling Museum	www.foundlingmuseum.org.uk
Galerie Ra	www.galerie-ra.nl
Galerie V&V	www.kunstnet.at
m2 Gallery	www.m2gallery.com
Museum of London	www.museumoflondon.org.uk
Pitt Rivers Museum	www.prm.ox.ac.uk
Rijksmuseum	www.rijksmuseum.nl
Wapping Project Gallery	www.thewappingproject.com

VIRTUAL GALLERIES

Chi ha paura...?	www.chihapaura.com
Contemp Art Jewels (1970-1988)	www.contempartjewels.com
Klimt 02	www.klimt02.net

Index